THE WAY OUT

Escape The Grind.
Make Money.
Get a Life!

Brendan Nichols

Published by Brendan Nichols Events
Email: info@brendannichols.com

1st Edition ISBN:
978-0-6452219-0-9 (paperback)
978-0-6452219-1-6 (eBook)

If you have an enquiry about speaking, bulk-order purchase or support, contact:
info@brendannichols.com

The paper in this book is FSC® certified. FSC® promotes environmentally responsible, socially beneficial and economically viable management of the world's forests.

Table of Contents

I was an idiot...

I remember the exact moment I became an idiot. Strangely enough, becoming an idiot was to change my life and create extraordinary success.

Let me briefly backtrack, so you can better understand my 'idiot moment'—the moment that led to my making millions as an entrepreneur.

I got out of school (yes, I did pass, much to the amazement of my teachers who knew I had little interest) and hit the road. You've heard of a gap year? Well, I had a gap decade, traveling the world on my endless summer, surfing enormous waves in Hawaii, Africa and remote Polynesia. I was funding it by entrepreneurial adventures—buying artwork in Madagascar, selling posters on the streets of Johannesburg and Sydney. It was a lot of fun until I became an idiot.

After finishing my travels around the world, my idiot moment arrived when I was taken to a small real estate office that had gone broke twice—that should have been a clue. I was told by the owner, who had another real estate business, that I could take over the office and make it an outstanding success. I had zero experience in real estate (clue number two). The business was an empty shell and the office had been closed for months (clue number three). The owner told me it would be my business; I could take a big percentage of the profits, but I would also incur all the losses (clue number four).

Believe it or not, I thought this was a good idea! It didn't occur to me that there wasn't actually a business to take over (hmmm, the clues just keep piling up, don't they?). But it gets worse... the office was four kilometers from the main shopping center, stuck in a tiny complex with only five other shops, eight parking spaces and NO walk-in traffic. I said YES... what the hell was I thinking?

To make it worse, my wardrobe looked like an image consultant's nightmare—no suit, one tie and two pairs of polyester business trousers. One was worth $19 and the other $17. I remember the prices because I had so little money that I bought the cheapest things I could find. In spite of all that, I was convinced this was my lucky break. What I lacked in common sense and business experience, I made up for with enthusiasm. At least, I did at the start. After the first month, I had no sales, was up to my eyeballs in debt, worked 12-hour days, and had a wife and a three-year-old daughter that had followed the idiot on this wild adventure—which now seemed destined for oblivion. We were so poor that we slept on a secondhand, faded red, fold-out lounge. 'Fold-out lounge' isn't really accurate—it didn't fold out flat, more as a shallow V. Think it can't get worse? Well, it does...

I still remember sitting in the kitchen of my two-bedroom rented house late at night. I was slumped over the old table, my elbows resting on the cracked Formica top and my head in my hands. I felt like I'd been hit by a truck. I looked up from the table, but the room was dark and empty. I felt very alone as the gravity of the situation landed.

2

I was the sole breadwinner in the family, and we had no bread. I was confused because I was working hard, but there was something else I felt. Something that bubbled up from inside, like a dark, murky cloud. Shame. I felt deeply ashamed that I had let my family down, but I felt something more—a failure. I started looking back at what I'd done to try and find some answers and see if there was something I was missing.

I felt desperate, and that I had hit the wall. The rage welled up inside me like a volcano. I thought, 'I've had it, I'm not putting up with this anymore, I have to change something!' I'd reached what I now call my Snap Point, and there was just no way I was going to let myself or my family down. I was working like a dog for no money, and I was going to find a way to reverse the situation if it killed me.

And I did. A few days later, a guy walks into my office and says he's looking for a house. As he's talking my ears prick up. 'Are you from Mauritius?' I ask.

He beamed from ear to ear. 'How could you possibly know that? I have lived here for years and most people have never heard of the island.'

'I lived there during my travels.'

The rapport between us was so strong, that an hour later he bought a house—my first sale! This gave me the confidence to try different approaches, because what I had been doing up to that point sure wasn't working. When I looked around, it seemed like everyone was doing business in the same kind of way. With nothing to lose, I started doing things in the business that no one was doing at the time. Things that most people thought were left of leftfield (more on that later). And it paid off.

Three and a half months after starting that business, we were making more sales than anyone in the area. Then it was on to bigger things. Eventually I moved into an office in the city, doing big projects, full-page ads in national newspapers and hanging out with business heavyweights—by then it was a serious business. I was known as a very successful troubleshooter, taking on difficult developments and turning them around.

So business was humming, yet something was missing. I felt I was very good at what I did, but it never felt like me.

I felt like I was wearing a glove that didn't fit. One day I was invited by a world-famous trainer to speak onstage. He asked me to talk on how I had achieved such remarkable success. Everything changed. I finally felt, as a speaker, I had something unique to share. You see, by then I had been to a lot of seminars and trainings, but the message was always similar—work, work, work, then work some more. When I looked around, I saw that most people were what I call 'grinders', doing long, long hours. However, I was doing something very different. Instead of working like a dog, then retiring when you're old and nearly dead, I was on a unique path. For over 30 years I have averaged more than three months vacation a year, holidaying in some of the most exotic places in the world. I wanted to develop 'passive income freedom' AND have a life at the same time. The idea of killing myself working, without having an actual life, was not my idea of a good time. Success is great but not at the expense of having a life. You CAN do both!

I have a saying, 'The only purpose to money is to get a life and give a life.' If you want to use money to feel better about yourself or superior to others it won't bring you long-term happiness. Money's only purpose is to allow you to have an amazing life and give an amazing life to others less fortunate than you are. I formulated a system of how you can make a lot of money and have an amazing life. Then I taught that around the world.

I told you I was an idiot. It turns out I am in good company. There is a little bit of an 'idiot' in most entrepreneurs. Ask the people who have outrageously successful businesses how many well-meaning people tried to talk them out of it in the beginning and be 'sensible'. They didn't have a perfect business plan, but what a lot of the really good ones had in common was something that distinguished them from the rest. I am going to show you these unique qualities in the following pages.

This book is about what I have found from my own journey, as well as the decades of research I have done to create a system that I have taught to tens of thousands of people around the world.

If you don't want to be a grinder, and want a business venture that is both a success and allows you to have a life, then I believe the following pages will reveal to you a revolutionary new approach to achieving just that. This was how I found 'The Way Out'.

There's something that's rarely discussed...

Most books about entrepreneurs, or the rich, focus on what they do—but what they do comes from who they are! If you want to win the Monaco Grand Prix, you are never going to do it in a clapped-out, $2,000-car—you need a Ferrari. The first thing you need are the five elements that create extraordinary success that turn you into a Ferrari—a person who is capable of winning the Grand Prix of life. There are five elements in this code. If you want to get to the top more easily, I believe it is essential to have a mix of all of them. If you are not willing to do that, then it is crucial to hire people who can cover your weak suits. Let's look at a brief summary of all five elements.

1. The Architect

The Architect of Your Dreams

Element—EARTH

Here is a fact for you: the journey has obstacles and if you don't have a very big 'WHY'—why you are doing it—then it's very difficult to get to the end.

Imagine you wanted to build a house. All the materials are piled up on the site ready to go, but the workers start without a plan—the house will look a mess! You need an Architect first. The Architect is the part of yourself that knows the plan. However, The Architect knows something more still—something that is vital. The Architect knows something that provides endless motivation.

Your Architect provides you with your purpose and your gift to the world. Like the element of earth, your internal Architect is a grounding influence in your life and gives you a sense of meaning. The Architect is also about the vision of what you want to create in the future for yourself. For many people, it's about getting to a place where they no longer need to work for money again. Where working is a choice.

WARNING: The Architect is about playing a bigger game and not hiding in the shadows, where there is little chance of significantly increasing your income. However, before you work yourself into a frenzy, growing some monster business that becomes your personal nightmare, bear this in mind: I knew someone who had a really profitable business. He hired a consultant who told him that business was all about growth, so he got a bigger building, more staff and stuff, worked his butt off and made not an iota of profit. Sometimes building a monster business with the big sign on the even bigger building works, but only IF it helps you create a LIFE. This book is written by someone who has been in the trenches, not an academic. Having trained thousands of entrepreneurs, I can say that most walk in the door with one thing in common: they don't have a life, they have a job—and it consumes them. The Architect creates an overall vision of how your working life is going to create an actual life.

The Architect is also about defying an age-old myth—that it's all about the money. I have been fortunate enough to mix with some great business leaders. For them, money is important, but it isn't just about the money. It's about doing something great or building something of significance. I have met a lot of wealthy people. While money is important to them all, I cannot think of a single one of them who started out to just make money. It was always something more—either a personal challenge, building something extraordinary or making a contribution. Someone who struggles with money once said to me, 'When are you going to stop working, surely you have enough now?' She doesn't get it. If you love something, why would you stop? One of the reasons she does not have a lot is because she thinks it's just about the money—it is about creating and making a difference.

Want more motivation?

The source of endless motivation is to discover why you are doing something. It's very easy to make yourself food if you are hungry. I remember consulting a confused, tired businesswoman who had been clocking up big hours—she was, sadly, a grinder. She had been in the doldrums for several months and her business was in decline. When I sat down with her, I asked why she was in business. She looked at me and said, 'Well, I need to pay the bills.' Obviously, this was not an inspiring point of view for herself or her employees. Over the course of several weeks, we established her vision, and the business began to flourish. You need a powerful vision to create powerful results. That vision has to inspire you. A vision creates a compelling picture of the financial life you wish to create for your future.

2. The Achiever

Fanning the Fire of Success
Element—FIRE

The Achiever is the part of you that goes for the goal—your outcome. A friend of mine who competes in sport at a very high level often tells me right before an event that he's 'on fire'. Like fire, Achievers burn their way to their goal. They see what they want, and they go for it.

With persistence and drive there is almost no height too great for an Achiever to scale. They love to challenge themselves and are often fiercely competitive.

The war cry of the achiever is 'results, results, results!' They know how to reach an outcome. However, more importantly, they know how to take action. I have seen so many people who 'prepare' for success. By all means study and learn; however, financial success comes to those who take action. There is simply no success without it. The Architect becomes inspired by the lofty vision of scaling Everest. The Achiever gets you to the top. It takes the dream and makes it a reality.

Years ago, I had a consultation with a couple, both in their mid-thirties. Sally, who I was meeting for the first time, looked at me with a teasing smile and said, 'I have a bone to pick with you.' Pointing at Bill her husband, she said, 'I have been trying to motivate him for the last four months and you were able to do what I failed to do in a single weekend.' Bill was an investment consultant who for the last few months had not been taking action. All I had done was get him clear on his vision (the Architect) and then got him to take action (the Achiever). I think a lot of motivational seminars are short-term fixes because all you are doing is awakening the Achiever. However, if you don't have a big WHY, it's probably not going to last.

3. The Poet

Having Fun and Loving Life
Element—WATER

A lot of people say that to succeed you should work 80 hours a week. When I speak to those people, they turn out to be centerline Achievers. Instead of working hard, work smart; we'll get to that in a while—a strategy to cut down your work and earn more. But for now, I want to address something crucial. You can get there and have fun along the way. And if you have fun, two things are going to happen. First, you are a lot less likely to burn out, and secondly, you won't be so miserable to be around. The people around you are more likely to love you, instead of despising you. LOVE—we are not supposed to talk about that word. Strive, conquer, achieve—it's okay to talk about those words. However, love works. You can love people and not be a pushover too. It's not only okay to love what you do and love your clients, it makes really good sense. I love helping people who want to be helped. I ran one particular mentoring group for many years where people paid thousands to belong. We always got over 93% re-enrolment every year and I think the reason for that boiled down to a few things. The information was cutting-edge, it created results, and people sensed that not only did we genuinely care about them, we also wanted them to win in their life.

No two elements are as opposite to each other as the Poet and the Achiever, just as water and fire are opposites. Like the nurturing qualities of water, the Poet nurtures you and your loved ones. A plant without water eventually shrivels and dies.

Deborah is a classic Poet. She also has a problem. Everyone in our local area says that Deborah brings laughter and sunshine wherever she goes. At work she is always trying to bring people together and create harmony. She seems to have a dozen things going at any given time, from assisting at the local school to baking cookies for a friend who needs cheering up. And that is her problem too. She has no direction, no Architect, very little Achiever, and she has no money! Are you starting to get the picture? Balance. Poets love life, people and expressing their creativity, however if that is all they have, then they will move from one thing to another and never achieve their potential.

The Poet is all about being in the moment. It is spontaneity, joy, love and innocence. If you would like to see the Poet in action, follow the movements of a small child. If you could condense the nature of the Poet in one word, it would be Heart.

While the Achiever is constantly trying to reach a goal and is in a state of doing, the Poet is simply being in the moment. I think being an entrepreneur is often categorized by Hollywood as someone tough and ruthless. Guess what? Sometimes you do have to be tough. You also have to have times where it's fun *and you care about people*.

4. The Sage

Perception, Wisdom and Getting on the Fast Track
Element—AIR

A Jewish friend of mine told me the story of how his father emigrated from Europe to Australia in the 1930s. His father was 16 years of age when he began to feel a sense of impending doom as Hitler rose to power. He was assured by everyone that there was no danger, yet still this feeling gnawed within. He begged his family to move out of Europe, but they wouldn't listen. Against all logic, and motivated by this intuition, he finally decided to leave his homeland to travel to the other side of the world, Australia. It took a lot of courage as he boarded the train, saying his last farewells to his mother and father. He was leaving a familiar place and journeying into the unknown. As he waved goodbye to his parents, he had no idea that it would be the last time he would ever see them.

They were caught up in the horror of the Holocaust. His intuition had saved him from a similar fate.

As he grew up, all his friends used to refer to him as 'the wise old professor'. People who are imbued with the Sage

12

often have this air about them. It is this wisdom that gives them an edge in this world.

Often, they are able to sense opportunities that others miss. While the Achievers like to struggle their way up the mountain of success, the Sage looks for the easy path—and often finds it. They have great timing and an ability to find the road less struggled.

Sages are like air—they can be hard to grasp hold of—but this quality allows them to move into places beyond the physical. If you have ever had the experience of your mobile ringing and *knowing* who it was before you picked it up, you have been in touch with your own Sage. If you have ever walked into old churches or buildings and sensed a certain atmosphere that is not present outside, you have felt your Sage. It may not seem rational, yet you and others feel it.

In Western cultures, this particular element is often considered strange and illogical—especially by centerline Achievers. The irony is that most people I know who have achieved great success attribute much of it to 'a gut feeling'. I know a very successful Wall Street businessman whose favorite quote is 'got a hunch, bet a bunch!' Now, I'm not telling you to act only on your intuition; you need to do your due diligence. However, there are countless stories about people who disregarded their gut and rued the day.

Having consulted with many outstanding people, I have yet to meet any who do not regard intuition and gut instinct as an essential part of financial success. However, it's not just about gut instinct, but also the ability to think outside the square.

People who become very successful do so because they do things differently. All my financially successful friends have a touch of the 'maverick' in them. Having trained thousands of businesspeople, I can pinpoint the single greatest problem for 80% of businesses. They don't make enough money because they don't have enough clients or customers—which all comes down to marketing. Marketing is the arena of the Sage. It's the ability to do things differently and stand out from everyone else. It is often the area where I will spend the majority of time with my business clients.

The Sage is also about something that is crucial—taking the easy road. People who are just centerline Achievers can reach their goals, but they often do it the hard way—long hours and heavy workload. Here is the big thing: when I meet grinders, they are almost always Achievers, with very little Sage—we need to wake that Sage up to get out of the grind!

The Sage just wants to get to the destination with the least amount of drama and in the easiest possible way. The Achiever just blasts through brick walls. Sometimes you need to go through the wall, and a lot of times it is easier to go around the wall. Sages like to do things with ease and grace.

The Sage is all about making the right choices. Have you ever had an instinct that a particular person was untrustworthy and been proven correct? If I am right, you have probably had a few times where you did not listen to your intuition and wished you had. Me too.

Using the Elements to Breakthrough...

Let me give you an example of how the first four elements work. Someone once said that the difference between a rut and a grave is just a few feet, and in Janet's case this was true. She later confided to me that when she first came to my events she was deeply depressed and her thoughts were moving in a dark direction. She had a fledgling business that was going nowhere and taking up all her time. Money pressures sat on her shoulders like a dead weight. We quickly used the Architect to establish a vision—a strong 'why'— something that inspired her, that would break her out of just trying to survive.

What Janet already had was a strong Achiever—a fierce and determined will. That was her blessing and curse. She was a battler and achieved success through grinding her way uphill, using long, long hours. We gave her some strategies (the Sage), that were geared toward increasing cashflow and getting wins on the board without as much struggle. The weight of the world started to lift from her shoulders.

Janet's Poet had been buried so deep that laughter, spontaneity and joy were long gone. She started to look after herself more, which increased her energy and gave her a positive outlook on life. Years later, she no longer needs to work for money again—that is the Architect in play—a long-term vision of what you want for your future and for others. Even though she doesn't need to work for money, she still loves the game and wants to continue being an entrepreneur.

5. Spirit
No Element—Beyond All Elements

There is a small village in Afghanistan that was once called Ghazni. While it is almost unknown today, 1,000 years ago it was one of the richest cities in Asia. This vast wealth was due to its monarch, King Mahmud, who invaded India 17 times, stripping that country of its riches to fill his own treasury. On his deathbed he asked his courtiers to carry him on a palanquin through his numerous treasure rooms. On seeing this vast display, he was filled with remorse, not only for the countless people who had suffered at his hands, but also the realization that none of his accumulated riches were going with him into the life beyond. He requested that at his funeral, his hands be placed outside the casket with his palms upturned, to signify he was leaving this world with nothing.

I think sometimes we think we are going to be here forever. I have met a lot of wealthy people. Some are happy and some are damn miserable. Some don't have a life outside of work—their work is their life. Sad. We are put on this earth not just to make money. Yeah, it's fascinating being an entrepreneur and what money can give you is positively awesome. However, it isn't the whole picture. There is another part of you that needs to be nurtured if you want to be happy.

The fifth element is your own Spirit, or soul; your eternal, animating principle. Your Spirit is something beyond your senses, your body and your mind. As it is outside the realm of the physical, it has no elemental structure. I am often asked what Spirit feels like. When there isn't a single thought in your mind, when your emotions are still and when all you feel is a sense of *beingness*, you are in touch with your Spirit. To be in contact with your own Spirit is not a process of doing, it is a process of undoing. It is about taking the filters away from the light that emanates from within you and letting it shine. Embracing your Spirit is not a new philosophy—rather, it is an experience that enhances your particular religion or philosophy.

Let me give you an example of how this forever changed someone's life. We were secluded in a big open house in Colorado, surrounded by a dense green forest on all sides. It was midwinter and the snow was deep on the ground. We had taken a group to see a Native American elder by the name of Richard Running Deer, who had devoted his whole life to helping people. Richard was what is commonly known as a 'medicine man', although being very humble, he never referred to himself as that.

As Richard stood to speak, what was most obvious to the group was his deep, quiet presence. Physically he was very tall and large in a raw-boned way, but that was not what was so arresting about him. It was his eyes—truly windows to the soul. Those eyes were powerful and penetrating, yet free of judgment.

One of the members of our group, David, asked Richard about a recurring problem he had been experiencing for most of his life. For as long as he could remember, he was plagued by deep feelings of inadequacy and self-doubt. He had tried many different things to combat these feelings. He was extremely successful in his career and in the top 1% of income earners in his country. To many of his colleagues at work he seemed self-assured, but he knew a lot of it was just an act.

Richard quietly listened as David spoke, his head cocked slightly to one side. Then when David had finished talking about his dilemma, Richard looked right into his eyes and precipitated what was one of the biggest turning points in this man's life. As he looked into his eyes he simply said, 'You're okay.'

In that one moment something deep within awakened. David had an experience of his Spirit. He felt a deep peace and certainty flood through him. One soul looked to another soul and transmitted the eternal truth that beyond the ever-changing personality, we are, and always will be, okay.

Years later, David still talks about that powerful moment. For the first time that he could remember, he profoundly *knew* he was okay, and the realization has never left him.

Without accessing this most priceless aspect of yourself, you are confined to success only in the material world. It is fabulous to achieve great distinction, honor and wealth, but it is your Spirit that keeps it all in perspective. What you do in the world may be important and vital to others, yet still it is a game that one day must end.

Being in touch with your Spirit gives you a presence and a sense of peace that filters into every area of your life. It allows you to feel centered and calmer in your relationships and in the world. It also allows you to maintain your responsibilities without getting so caught up in the day-to-day world that you lose perspective on just how small your part is in the great game of life. This attitude creates more peace in your life, which actually makes you more effective in the world. Rather than worrying about unimportant things, your peace of mind lets you focus on the tasks that really matter. All of this actually helps you as an entrepreneur.

When I think of all the great rulers who have come and gone, and look at the countless stars in the heavens, it puts everything in perspective.

Did you know that there are more stars in the universe than there are grains of sand in all the deserts and beaches of the world?

Think about that for a moment. How many countless grains are in one handful of sand? When I tend to get caught up in some 'crucial' task, this reminds me that although each of our lives is important to the whole network of the universe, ultimately, we are tiny strands in that incredibly vast web.

Find Out Which Element You Are

Do the Free Quiz.

Go to:
www.TheFreeQuiz.com

Discover in one minute the hidden
patterns that can create success…

- This Quick Quiz Can Also Reveal Hidden Sabotage
  Patterns. Find out what could be holding you back.

- Discover the Code That Successful Entrepreneurs
  Use. At last, a totally different, and unique code that
  can show you an easier path to get to where you want
  to go.

Find Out How…

Go to www.TheFreeQuiz.com.

Embracing the Elements

We all have the five elements within us. We are the Sage, the Achiever, the Architect and the Poet, all wrapped around a timeless, eternal being known as our Spirit. We all possess the inherent tendencies of every element. We don't have to 'invent' these elements within us because they are already there. We merely have to develop them.

Before I move on to an in-depth analysis of each element and how you can use it to create extraordinary success, I will show you some practical examples of how the elements work together.

Imagine you had a business or a project you wanted to get off the ground. The Architect would come up with the idea, the inspiration and the vision. The Achiever would make sure the vision was started and completed. The Poet would ensure you had fun and inspired people's love and warmth in working with you. The Sage would be looking out for pitfalls and correct timing, and your Spirit would keep the whole project in perspective.

I once worked as a consultant for a big company whose people were primarily Poets. Everyone in the company said it was one of the warmest and most caring environments they had ever worked in, yet the common complaint was that very little was achieved. People talked about change and financial progress but not much ever happened. The owner was quietly pulling his hair out because there wasn't a lot of money coming in the door.

Like all Poets, they loved the process itself, rather than achieving the goal. On the other hand, I have also worked with companies who are full of Achievers, where bitching was high, trust and caring were low and mistakes were frequent. You need both elements to be activated—in fact all of them—for a long-term, unshakeable success.

How the Elements Work in the Real World

The following diagram represents a wheel. For a wheel to travel smoothly over the ground it needs to be a complete circle. When all five elements come together, the circle is complete, creating a smooth ride through the journey of your life. The center or hub of the wheel is your Spirit. When you or a business achieves this balance, it looks like this:

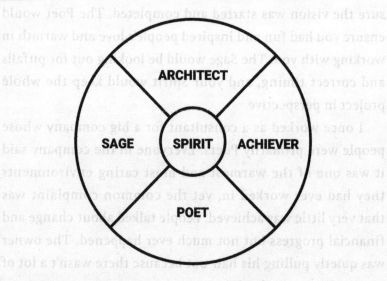

Now let's look at what your wheel would look like with one of the elements missing:

If you were undeveloped in the element of the Poet, you would have difficulties relating to people. Others might perceive you as abrasive or distant. You might respond with caution and a lack of trust. It would be difficult for the wheel to turn over the missing piece. You would be in for a bumpy ride.

Take another piece out of the wheel and the problem would be compounded. If you lacked both the Poet and the Achiever, your ride would be even more uncomfortable than someone who is undeveloped in just the Poet aspect. Projects would never get off the ground, or if they did, things would slowly grind to average as you struggled to find personal motivation. If we took another element out of the picture, imagine how that would complicate matters even further. The wheel of life would have great difficulty in turning at all! This is why so many people struggle in life and business.

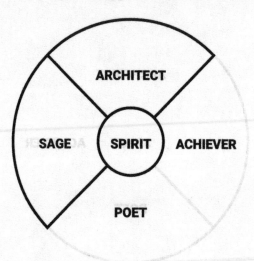

Let's now delve deeper into each element and discover how to springboard into greatness.

The Five
Elements

The Architect

*"Some men see things as they are and say, why? I
dream of things that never were and say, why not?"*
—GEORGE BERNARD SHAW

The Dreaded Dead Zone

It was like a scary scene from a horror movie, except this was
real life. I was in Sydney as part of a national tour, which
involved speaking every evening in a different city.

I was due on stage in a few hours and was looking through
some of my latest research, and decided to go for a walk to stretch my
legs before getting ready. As I closed the door, I noticed it was just
before five o'clock. It briefly crossed my mind that it might be busy but
I left the room anyway. As I approached the train station at Wynyard
I realized 'busy' didn't come close to the mayhem in progress.

I could see two of my promoters busily distributing flyers
about that night's event, but that wasn't what caught my
attention. I was reminded of those terrible B-movie zombie
horror flicks from the 1960s. I'd just stumbled into the Dead
Zone—only this was real life!

Thousands of tired, disinterested, miserable-looking
people filed past me. There was no life in their eyes, no

conversation, no gentleness or kindness and certainly no smiles or laughter. Everyone seemed to be operating on autopilot, focused solely on getting to the couch and the remote control as quickly as possible. And this was them leaving work—I dread to think how thrilled they must have looked in the morning!

They all had one big thing in common: no Architect. No vision or purpose.

Wynyard train station is not unique. I could have been standing in any station in any town or city around the world. In fact, my work as an international speaker takes me to all corners of the globe. The Dead Zone is alive and well from New York to London to Budapest to Singapore. It is made up of millions of people in jobs they hate, just going through the motions. It's burnt-out business owners trying to pay the bills. The Dead Zone is where people feel trapped by the circumstances of their life, with no hope for a better solution. It is where wealth and freedom are a lifetime away, and nothing more than a dream.

I know what it's like to have been there. I remember one night a long, long time ago staying in my office until 11 o'clock and feeling so exhausted that I literally fell asleep in my office chair. I woke up in the wee hours of the morning with a stiff back and bloodshot eyes that felt like they were hanging out of my head. I know what it is like to wonder, 'Will it ever happen? Can I ever escape the rat race?'

I am fortunate enough to have lived my life on my own terms for a long time now. I don't do rush hour. I conduct my business around my schedule. I'm not prepared to crawl through city traffic to get to a job I hate. I'm not interested in watching the lights turn green in front of me again, having moved only two inches as I'm on my way to a meeting with a client I neither like nor respect. There is no way I'm going to squash myself into a humid train carriage in the height of summer. I'm certainly not interested in missing my children's special moments because I'm tied up in strategy meetings or working out how to keep the bank manager at bay for another month. And what's the point of being in a relationship if the only conversation you have time or energy for is what to watch on the screen that night, and you can't even remember when you last went out together or shared a really good laugh! Basically, I'm not interested in battling my way through life so I can reach some mystical future milestone where easy street magically opens up. My guess is neither are you—or you wouldn't be reading this book.

How to Use the Architect to Build Massive Motivation

"While there is no vision, the people perish."
—PROVERBS, 29.18

What would happen if I put a whole lot of building equipment on a vacant block of land and asked you to build a house without a plan? It would be a complete disaster. Without detailed architect's drawings, it would be a mess.

You may think this is a cliché, but seriously, why should your life be any different? I am always staggered at how few people put their internal Architect to work. How is it that you would think it ridiculous to attempt to build a house without a detailed plan, and yet most people attempt to build a life or build a successful business without one!

Your internal Architect is the part of you that develops a vision of where you want to go.

Purpose and Vision Always Precede Goals

The most important word in the English language is 'why'. 'Why' is the reason you do everything—you ate breakfast this morning because you had a 'why'. Hunger.

If you want to make a lot of money, or do something substantial, you need a strong enough 'why' to get you to the goal. You need a 'why' to stay motivated, and the Architect is the part of you that gives you that WHY.

One time a guy, by the name of David, stood up in one of my seminars. He looked sheepish as about 600 sets of eyeballs focused their attention on him. Realizing he had the floor, he jumped in. 'I've got a problem.' His nerves momentarily overcame him and he looked toward the ceiling and then at me. I gave him a warm encouraging smile and a nod.

He continued. 'I have some big moments of success, but I seem to constantly go through big troughs and valleys.' I looked at him and said, 'You mean ups and downs in your motivation?' Looking relieved, he kept going. 'Yeah, exactly. It's so frustrating. I have been to lots of motivation seminars trying to fix it. I just don't know why I stop and start.'

When you have been doing what I have been doing for as long as I have, often you know what the person's problem is just by looking at them. However, it is often better for them to discover it for themselves. Giving him a mischievous grin I cheekily said, 'David, would you like to do something a little off the wall?'

He stiffened. 'Sure.' The room laughed in a good-natured way at his discomfort, and he seemed to relax.

'David, I promise I won't bite.'

He nodded his head vigorously. 'Okay, I'm in.'

Turning to the crowd, I said, 'David has to do everything I say for the next few minutes and every time he starts a task you have to wildly cheer him on, just like you would if you were in a motivation seminar.'

I then picked up a pen and threw it about seven meters away from David. The pen hit the floor and rolled along the carpet. Looking at David I said, 'David, quick, run and get the pen!' David scooted off and immediately brought the pen straight back to me. The audience cheered and clapped at his performance.

Without giving him a chance to pause, I threw the pen and repeated the command, 'Quick David, run and get the pen!' David took off in a sprint and once more retrieved the pen. The audience of course applauded and screamed their approval. I repeated this for several minutes. By now David was beginning to look confused, so I asked him what he was thinking. David replied, 'Well I am beginning to wonder why the hell I am doing this.'

'David, is this a little bit like your life? You start with a full head of steam and then run out of puff?'

31

He went quiet for a moment. 'Absolutely.'

I continued. 'The reason you have a problem with this exercise of getting the pen, is because you think it's stupid. You can't see any point to it. And you are right, it is stupid and pointless because there is no reason for doing it.'

I explained to him that his problem was a common one. He had set his goals and had made progress up to a certain point but he never had a strong enough 'why' once the initial motivation wore off. He didn't have a purpose that backed up his goals.

I am sure, like David, you have experienced hitting what I call the 'why brick wall'. You've been running down the road of life and all of a sudden you've asked, 'Why the hell am I doing this?'

An Extraordinary Experience

I was in Venice many years ago and wandered down some winding, twisting, cobblestone back alley. As I rounded the corner, there in front of me was the most exquisite cafe, decked out in deep mahogany timber and polished brass fittings. The waiters all wore spotless white coats and silk bowties. I was greeted by a waiter who gave me the most extraordinary service. He treated me as if he really cared (as opposed to acting like he cared). You know, I cannot remember what I ate that day, but I remember him. I believe I still have the card of that restaurant tucked away in one of my drawers.

Everything there is done with a sense of perfection and every guest is treated like a king or queen. It isn't an act with them, it's genuine. What makes this place so special is that they have a vision to create an extraordinary experience. This goes way beyond good customer service—they create an experience! That is the 'why'; and their 'how' is by delivering, among other things, fabulous food and unforgettable service.

The trouble with goal-based motivation is that it's short-lived. In the old days with my sales teams before I knew any better, I would take them to motivational seminars and they'd get really revved up. Everybody would leave feeling as though they were going to take over the world. Then I'd watch as that initial enthusiasm and passion would drain away—often leaving them feeling flatter than they had been before we went to the event!

Finally, what I came to realize is that the fundamental driving force of passion, and hence motivation, is PURPOSE. You've got to have a purpose—your 'why'.

If you don't, you will constantly feel these highs and lows of motivation! If you have a purpose, on the other hand, you have a big enough 'why' to sustain you through those natural ups and downs. You are able to bring everything you do back to some simple home truths about who you are and what you want to do in your life. Having a powerful purpose is the hallmark of excellence in any field.

Who's Keeping the Flame Alive?

Think of it like this. When some indigenous tribes would go walking for long distances, they would assign one person to be the keeper of the flame. As you can imagine, there were times when it was very difficult to make a fire. So the person who was assigned this role would take a smoldering piece of coal, or something that kept the flame alive, and their sole job was to keep the flame burning. Perhaps it would be better described as their 'soul job'! When you discover your purpose or assign yourself a purpose, you are keeping the fire alive in your soul.

When our flame goes out, we are in big trouble because then we don't know why we are doing what we are doing, and we lose our way and our motivation. But with a strong-enough 'why' and a powerful enough purpose, we can always navigate ourselves back on track.

Often the big focus in seminars is on setting goals. And sure, you do have to know what it is you're trying to achieve, and goals are important, but goals are always secondary to purpose.

Goals without purpose are as potent as the average new year's resolution! And we all know how many of them come to fruition.

Your internal Architect determines your purpose. Yes, improving your own life is one driving purpose—and completely valid—however, if that's all you've got in your arsenal, it usually isn't strong enough to get you to your goal. One of the most powerful purposes always seems to involve helping other people. Human nature dictates that we will always do more for those we care about than we will do for ourselves. A purpose that makes other peoples' lives easier, better, or happier in some way is a strong motivating force. When there is a deeper meaning to your actions, that wellspring of motivation can be tapped whenever you feel jaded by your goals.

There are always going to be ups and downs in your life. If there weren't, you'd be dead! Having a purpose or a grand vision, however, makes the navigation of those ups and downs easier. Without that, you may find yourself in a low, and not have the motivation or the pull to move you through it.

As Viktor Frankl, author of *Man's Search for Meaning* and survivor of the Nazi concentration camps, wrote, 'A man who becomes conscious of the responsibility he bears toward a human being who affectionately waits for him, or to an unfinished work, will never be able to throw away his life. He knows the "why" for his existence, and will be able to bear almost any "how".'

This is also crucial if you want to be a leader. If you don't want to do this all on your own, you are going to need a team. To inspire others, you need a vision. If we think of great leaders throughout history, they inspired people through a shared purpose. Even if you outsource a lot of the work, the right people are going to feel way more motivated if they are a part of something that is adding value.

Let's take this a step further...

Two Steps to Discovering Purpose and Increasing Income

STEP 1: Your Grand Purpose

I was once asked if I was a motivator. 'No,' I replied. 'I get people in touch with their own motives so that they can motivate themselves.'

Most people who seem to wander through their lives aimlessly aren't lazy—they don't have a purpose. When you find your purpose, you never have to worry about being motivated again. You automatically know where you are going. Every morning your feet hit the deck and there is a clear mission of what your life is about.

The first step in finding your overall purpose is to discover what the Architect recognizes as a higher level of motivation or direction.

This higher level is known as your Grand Purpose. Realizing this is step one.

Everyone has the same Grand Purpose. It is this: to grow and evolve. People might use different words to say the same thing: some might say they are here to be a bigger person, or a better person, or to fulfill their potential, or achieve great things.

Monster, an employment agency, did an ad during a Super Bowl that was to become a huge hit. The ad, shot in black and white, shows kids looking directly into the camera and talking in a deadpan delivery 'When I grow up I want to file all day... When I grow up I want to climb my way up to middle management... I want to have a brown nose... When I grow up I'll do anything for a raise.' The ad was a big hit—a lot of people could relate to being stuck in a dead-end job that provides no challenges and no avenue for growth, and leads to giving up on your dreams. It spoke to a lot of people and gave Monster an enormous boost in growth. We are hard-wired to grow and evolve—our Grand Purpose. It is who we are. Part of that Grand Purpose is also adding value to others.

I have felt from an early age that my Grand Purpose is simply my personal evolution, and that my task is to constantly grow. Any action I take that leads me towards that Grand Purpose means I am on track. Any action that leads me away from it means I am off track. It is that simple. And that doesn't mean I have always been on track. That is how we learn sometimes. Going in the wrong direction can teach us valuable lessons.

Let's say you absolutely know the primary reason you are here on Earth is to grow and evolve. You know that there is more to life than just existing and paying the bills. Congratulations, you have achieved step one of becoming more of the Architect. Now you need a Vehicle to make that Grand Purpose a reality.

STEP 2: Finding a Vehicle That Makes Money—THE HARD TRUTH
An entrepreneurial venture is one arena that provides us with a Vehicle where we can fulfill our Grand Purpose—to grow and evolve. Often people begin a new business with a big head of steam and feeling excited about the challenge, and then run into a 'money brick wall'. Social entrepreneurs wishing to help the world leap in with great intentions. For quite a few, they become jaded as they struggle to make money. I have met so many people who believe you can either add value, or make money, but not do both—that is a hoax. You CAN DO BOTH. Yes, you can truly care about people and make a big income.

So the question is, how do you channel that Purpose into a Vehicle that makes money? And what kind of Vehicle, you ask? Time to get real. It needs to be 'commercially realistic'. Ever heard of the saying, 'Do what you love and the money will follow?'

Is it true? Yes and no. Here is where it's a hoax. I really love skiing. I'm really passionate about it, so if I decide to do that for the rest of my life then I'll take a collection from you, wonderful reader, so that you can support me doing what I love... What do you think? Do you like the idea? Yeah, I didn't think so.

No one is going to pay you to do what you love, unless what you love serves what they want. The only way to make money is to add value, to make someone's life better, easier or happier in some way. That's the reality of human nature. Now, don't get me wrong—you also have to love what you do to succeed. However, just because you love it, that doesn't mean it's necessarily commercially realistic.

Let me give you an example of something that was very commercially realistic—even though I was not head-over-heels in love with it. I was a trouble-shooter in real estate, specializing in selling big developments for developers that were often in trouble. I was very good at it. I loved aspects of it, but it never felt like me. It felt like a glove that I had put on that did not quite fit. Despite it not being my ideal glove, I still made money from it and it was an amazing stepping-stone into what I do now. If you are in something that doesn't quite fit, I want to sound a word of warning.

Will Cucumbers Make You Rich?

People say to me something like, 'Brendan, you know I realize the business that I'm in is wrong and I'm not passionate about it anymore. I've got this new passion. I've decided that I'm going to grow cucumbers. I've got the most amazing cucumbers in the world and I'm going to unleash my cucumbers on the planet because everybody wants a cucumber.'

Trust me, the world is not on tenterhooks waiting for your cucumbers. Most people couldn't care less about your cucumbers! Let me give you a quick, real-life example. I was walking through a nearby town with my wife, when I spotted a new store that sold fudge—dozens of different types of fudge. My only comment was four words; 'broke in two months.' I was wrong—it was six weeks. The owner loved his fudge; sadly he was the only one. Am I saying you should not be passionate about what you do? Of course not, passion is important—but just make sure it is something other people are passionate about buying.

Test it! Find out if somebody actually wants your fudge or cucumbers.

Let's take a step back for a second and get a reality check. No one—I don't care who they are or what they're doing—no one loves what they do all the time. We all have to do things we don't want to: it's called 'being an adult'. I am very fortunate to love what I do.

I have one client whom I have coached and he's now rich. He is about to sell his business for approximately $9 million and I can tell you he was never in love with it. Now he wants to find what he loves, and that's okay. It's also easier with $9 million in the bank!

'Do what you love and the money will follow' is only half-true. It's popular in new-age seminars or personal development reveries, and while the idea is sound in principle, it's only half the story. So by all means, explore working in areas that interest you and move your business into areas that you are passionate about BUT only if you've done the research and you know there's a market for it.

Once upon a time I was deluded...

There is one more important thing I want to add about following your dream and changing the world. It's embarrassing to admit, but in the beginning I actually felt that going out and trying to help people change their lives was far more noble than my previous business, and that now I was truly adding value. Crap! I hear a lot of social entrepreneurs talk in a demeaning way about people in a 'regular' business. It's just the ego trying to feel special and different.

Let me give you a classic example. Pam Elardo heads up the New York City sewage and wastewater treatment. Every day she works in the least sexy industry you could think of—crap! The city generates over a billion gallons of wastewater every day—the engineering effort is monumental. It's something we take for granted. Pam and her team's efforts are dissed by some environmentalists, and yet Pam is mind-blowingly passionate about crap—or at least the ability to dispose of it. She believes they are saving lives. Think that is an overstatement? According to *The British Medical Journal*, the biggest medical breakthrough in the last 150 years is sanitation. Pam knows this first-hand, from watching kids die when she was working in the Peace Corps in Nepal. They died of dysentery and other diseases due to lack of sanitation. Pam passionately believes that every day when she goes to work she and her team are saving lives! That recognition of what her job is about gives her a huge edge and provides a big boost of passion and motivation.

Adding value is simply helping people and recognizing that. The waitperson who brings you coffee is adding value to your day. However, here is the kicker: if they recognize that, like Pam, the value goes up exponentially. Who would you rather bring you coffee: a person who thought it was just a job, or someone who thought they were adding value to your life? The bus driver who gets people to their destination is just as valid as the social entrepreneur—we are all in service. When we add value to someone, we are serving them. When we recognize that, our life takes on meaning.

Your vision will usually present itself in one of two ways. It will most likely be something that you are extremely passionate about, or something that frightens you—sometimes both. That was true in my case. I was originally terrified of speaking in public. There are two kinds of fear. The first is healthy fear—for example, being frightened of jumping out of a plane without a parachute. Healthy fear keeps us alive. The second is obstructive fear, fear that you need to push through, fear that is merely an obstruction in your path.

When you choose something that challenges you, it shapes you and allows you to grow, thus fulfilling your Grand Purpose of constant evolution. However, there is something that can stop you. It's the big scary monster...

Staring Down the Big Scary Monster

Janice was a client who was living at half her potential. She owned and operated a business that designed, made and retailed exclusive women's clothing. When she first came to see me she was quite despondent. Her business had been struggling for many years and barely made a profit. When I examined her clothing range, it was clear to me she had a fantastic product. However, her problem wasn't in the clothes or the design. The problem was Janice. She was allowing her fear of what others thought about her to keep her small, and this was reflected in her marketing. All her marketing efforts were written in an almost apologetic style. Her marketing did not reflect the quality of her designs; rather, it portrayed the designs as almost ordinary. After some discussion, we agreed that I would rewrite her marketing for a series of upcoming showings. When I finally delivered the marketing piece she was mildly aghast. 'Brendan,' she said, 'this makes me look vain. People will think I'm arrogant.' I knew that the marketing piece was honest and direct and delivered the truth of her product. I looked at her and simply asked, 'Are you going to let what other people think of you determine how far you are going to fly in life?' That was her Big Scary Monster— what other people thought. There was a long pause. Finally she said, 'You're absolutely right. I have this vision of where I want to go in my life and business and I am the one that's standing in the way.'

Plucking up her courage, she decided it was finally time to stand out and stare down the Big Scary Monster. The result was that all her showings were completely sold out for six solid weeks. The business completely turned around and so did Janice. She decided to play a bigger game.

The Bigger Game
When Janice decided to put herself out there, she was being courageous and playing a bigger game. Which leads us to a very interesting story...

Imagine you live in a wonderful place, in a far-off, distant land. In this paradise, whenever you tell any of your friends or family about your dreams to be rich and successful, they applaud and cheer. When you post about your latest success, you receive 100% positive comments. Everyone on social media is overjoyed that you made millions in your latest venture. If this place actually existed I probably wouldn't have a job.

There are loads of people who will either directly or subtly want to stop you having a financial win or achieving a big goal. I have asked hundreds of people this question: 'What is the annual income of the five closest friends you have?' Let's say someone in the audience yells out that all five of their closest friends make a certain figure. THERE IS SOMETHING EVEN MORE INTERESTING: they make a similar income to their five closest friends! More than 90% of people will make a similar income to their five closest friends. Birds of a feather flock together. And quite often when one bird flies high and doubles their income, the other birds in their group, want to clip their wings. Even more important is that often people choose to be accepted by their peers, rather than being judged and ostracized by their group. So they end up playing a game that is smaller than what they really want.

Traits That Self-Sabotage

What stops you from pursuing your Grand Purpose and your ideal Vehicle? One answer is what I call 'Small Reasons'.

Just as the urge to eat and drink is an instinct, your Grand Purpose for living is also an instinct. You have certain impulses so that you survive and thrive. Notice I said survive and thrive. You are not meant to just exist, but also to bloom.

If you want to satisfy your hunger and thirst instincts, all you need to do is eat bread and water. However, this is not a diet that will allow you to thrive. Similarly, there are millions of people working in businesses and jobs that satisfy their instinct to survive by providing income, but the instinct to thrive remains unsatisfied. They don't really like what they are doing, they are stuck in a rut. They are on the equivalent of bread and water rations and are not thriving.

You may think that slavery in the Western world is dead, but this is not the case. Slavery is alive and well. Instead of an external slave master, a huge number of people are self-imprisoned. They are their own slave master. They are being driven by Small Reasons, such as, 'I have to pay the bills' or 'What will my friends and colleagues think?'

Now, Small Reasons are important in life. You need to pay the bills and handle the details, but Small Reasons do not make up an inspiring Vehicle or a Grand Purpose. Small Reasons relate to management, and this shouldn't be confused with the Architect. Management refers to handling the day-to-day running of your life and business, and that is important. The Architect is the dream that inspires you. A manager of a family or a business looks after all the very important details, the Small Reasons. A leader creates the vision. Many politicians are uninspiring because they are managers rather than leaders.

A Tragic Tale...

The impact of Small Reasons can be seen in the following story. There are countless people who secretly struggle to find fulfillment, and I have met many like Mary and Jonathan.

Mary and Jonathan had been in a relationship for seven years. Mary worked as a retail manager with a large supermarket chain. Jonathan was climbing the career ladder in a firm of engineers. When they first got together, the relationship was full of passion and they both felt alive. Jonathan had always nursed a dream that after finishing his degree he would take two years off and sail around the world. Mary was attracted to his heroic sense of adventure, for she had dreams and a vision of her own. She loved interior design and wanted to start her own company. They decided, however, to put their dreams on hold for just a little while and do the sensible thing. They would save up and buy a house.

Seven years went by. Mary often felt that she had missed her opportunity. Working in a supermarket was not quite her. It didn't really feel like it was what she was meant to be doing with her life.

In his quieter moments, Jonathan wondered what the hell he was doing in the engineering company. He had very little in common with his colleagues and he felt like an outsider.

It was as if he was scrambling to get to the top of a hill. The only problem was, it was the wrong hill.

When Mary and Jonathan talked about how they both felt stuck, there seemed too much pressure to change. Jonathan believed if he left the firm their income would stop. He reasoned their lifestyle would suffer and their friends would look down on them. He didn't like the thought of not being able to keep up. Mary wasn't willing to take the risk of giving up her job. They could lose the house, which would make her feel extremely insecure. He worried about what people would think of him, and she was willing to give up her dreams for the sake of security.

Both Mary and Jonathan were dominated by Small Reasons. They were not living with a Grand Purpose, but rather, with a whole host of Small Reasons. While they were both outgoing and well liked by all their friends, deep down they both felt something was missing in their lives. They didn't feel as alive as they used to. They did not feel inspired, nor did their partner inspire them.

Their relationship was suffering too. Their friends thought they had it all together, but they both knew they were becoming more distant and unfulfilled. They often felt as though they were just existing rather than thriving.

One of the biggest fears that people have is the fear of ostracism—the fear of being excluded from their particular community. Some people would twist themselves in knots rather than be ridiculed. The Architect, however, is willing to operate in 'non-agreement'. This is a state where you are willing to live a unique way of life and genuinely not care what people think.

When you can operate in non-agreement, you harness a huge amount of energy. This energy is often channeled into self-censorship. Wearing the right thing, saying the right thing, doing the right thing—absolutely exhausting. When you can just be yourself, you free yourself.

The Architect sits comfortably in their own skin.

Your Ongoing Journey

Your Grand Purpose is a constant and continues as you grow. However, your Vehicle can change to fulfill your Grand Purpose. Often to get to the next step you have to stare down another Big Scary Monster. When I first started my original business, my Big Scary Monster was the overwhelming challenge of it all. Then after that became easy, or normal, a new Vehicle arrived. When I first started as a speaker, I was terrified of talking in public—that was my Big Scary Monster.

A good way to think of how your Grand Purpose and your Vehicle relate to each other is to imagine you are sitting in the pilot seat of a jet. The jet is currently parked on the runway in Paris. Deep down inside, you recognize your Grand Purpose is to fly west. You decide to set a course to New York. Traveling westwards to New York is the Vehicle that helps you move closer to your Grand Purpose. Once you arrive at New York, this Vehicle is fulfilled. However, as your Grand Purpose is to fly west you need another Vehicle, so you decide to go to San Francisco. Once you are there, your Vehicle is complete, but has your Grand Purpose been fulfilled? No, so you set out westwards for Tokyo.

Just as your destinations will change, your Vehicles or projects will change over time. It might be the same business over 20 years, but new challenges or Vehicles will arrive to keep you growing. Something that you were extremely passionate about 10 years ago may no longer appeal to you today. In my case, I realized that I had to leave a successful business. If I was to keep evolving, my Vehicle had to change. As my passion for my project marketing company diminished, my passion for 'coming out' and speaking what I knew was growing. Fulfilling this Vehicle helped me to keep pursuing my Grand Purpose.

When your Architect is well developed, you become clear on what your vision is, and can recognize the difference between a true vision and a simple desire or wish for something. I wish I could sing as well as Andrea Bocelli, and I would love to play the guitar like Eric Clapton. The truth is, I'm not committed to these things because I don't have a strong enough motive, or talent!

Genuine passion is created by finding your Grand Purpose and discovering your unique Vehicle.

So You Want To Be Rich? The Quantum Income Leap—Your 'Success Drivers'

I think more people are hung up about money than any other issue. People speak so disparagingly of it and yet everyone wants it. As I have said, money is ONLY good for two things:

'Get a life and give a life.' It is to create a life for yourself and to create a life for others. It is to provide FREEDOM for you and your loved ones and for giving away to some great charities. That is its only purpose. If you are trying to create an image for yourself and impress others, then I think you are missing a big point. At the end of your life the only thing you take with you is the person you have become. The money stays here, so you might as well enjoy it while you are around and become a person you and the people you care about can be proud of. And you can do that and make money—you absolutely can do both.

Whether you achieve that or not depends on your Success Drivers.

IMPORTANT: *It is possible to have a Grand Purpose and the right Vehicle and still NOT make money. You can have the right Vehicle, but whether you make money depends a lot on your Success Drivers. I have taken thousands of people through this exercise and it is BIG wake-up call to many. When people get into any entrepreneurial venture they are motivated at a very deep level by a series of 'psychological drivers'. These drivers are usually unknown to them consciously. They sit below the surface of your conscious awareness and determine your future—they can determine whether you struggle or succeed.*

Here is the full list of the Success Drivers, in no particular order:

- *Recognition*
- *Fame*
- *Achievement*
- *Handling Survival* (the yearly amount to cover your total lifestyle and expenses)
- *Abundance of Money* (making far more than you need, creating a big surplus)
- *Satisfaction of a Job Well Done*
- *The Pursuit of Excellence*
- *Competition*
- *Empire Builders* (wanting to create a business empire)
- *Contribution to Humanity* (philanthropist)
- *Productivity/Busyness* (hard-working people who love to be busy and accomplish lots of things)
- *Creativity*
- *Praise*
- *Fun*

I have had people do the following exercise and sit in stunned silence as they realized why they struggle so much with their finances.

Take at look at these 14 psychological Success Drivers. I want you to go through the list and rank them in order of importance. Let's say you looked at the list and decided that the satisfaction of a job well done was your primary motivator at work. Write '1' next to that. If you're very competitive and are driven to be the best in everything you do, then competition is probably your number one Driver. Work down the list and allocate a rank to each Driver.

By the way, I'm not asking you what you want your Drivers to be, or what you hope they are or what you think your partner hopes they are or what they might be in the future. I'm talking about right now. Be honest—what is it about your work or your business that is really driving you?

I run this exercise in my seminars and I've literally had people cry once they found this out!

The Reality Bomb...

I vividly remember Lance. He was CEO of a big company, he had two secretaries, a monster-sized office and a big salary, but apart from owning his own home, he had nothing but a small super fund. He was around 50 years of age and had worked all his life. He was sitting there after doing this exercise and he looked like 'the reality bomb' had gone off in his head. He was stunned. He actually came up to me during the break and said, 'That was one of the most profound things I have ever done in my life. Now I know why I am successful but not wealthy! The thing that I care about most is recognition and the pursuit of excellence. All my life I have worked towards that, and funnily enough, that is exactly what I've got. I have been recognized and created excellent work. However, I spent most of my money on all the right toys because they got me recognition. And I never went into business for myself because I wanted recognition from the owners of the company.'

Just understanding what was really driving him was a relief for him. He'd worked hard and was genuinely good at his job.

He had always been confused as to why he couldn't translate that obvious ability into wealth. Now he knew, and because he knew, he was able to change his life.

Take a look at your list—I'm about to do something really amazing. I'm going to predict something that's going to blow you away. If you are currently not making as much money as you'd like—and let's face it, you wouldn't be reading this book if you were—then I'm going to dazzle you with my predictive powers... Drumroll please... Abundance of Money doesn't figure in your top two. Or, if Abundance of Money is your number one and you don't have a really strong number two, you won't make a lot of money either. People who ONLY want money don't usually have any—at least long-term. We will get to why later.

Here is the other thing I find often. If you need $80,000 a year to cover your entire lifestyle, or you need $250,000 a year to have that lifestyle, then often that is exactly what you will make. That is handling survival. Often people make exactly what they need but they never have enough to invest to get out of the rat race.

What I've found over and over again when I run this exercise in seminars is that those people who make serious money in business are the ones who have Abundance of Money usually in the first two of their priorities. It could be, for example, that Abundance of Money is number two and number one is Competition (or the other way around—money may be number one). Money is very often a by-product of what they do in order to meet their other higher-ranking Drivers. Or it could be money and another strong Driver.

These Success Drivers are psychological aspects of our nature. They represent what we really value. Very often, people are completely unaware of them, and yet are driven by them!

I will let you in on a secret. When I first started in business, my two Drivers were Recognition and Satisfaction of a Job Well Done. No wonder I didn't make any money! Because I was about to disappear into a financial abyss, I automatically made money a priority. I had to—it was sink or swim.

These days my two key motivators are very different. Contribution to Humanity and Abundance of Money are at the top of the list. As far as Contribution to Humanity goes, that is very specific. Sure, I donate money to charities, however, that is not where I believe my biggest contribution is. Several years after she began coming to my seminars, Janet told me that when she first arrived, she was thinking of suicide—her business and life were a disaster. Along with doing a number of things, she changed her Drivers. Now she is a multi-millionaire and thriving in business and her personal life.

Busy But Broke?

Take Susan, for example: she came to a lot of my seminars and was one of the hardest-working people I had ever met. She loved achieving goals and being incredibly busy and she easily did the work of two people. But she found it really hard to make money from her business. When she prioritized her drivers, she realized that Productivity/Busyness was number one and recognition was number two. Money was nowhere in sight.

This is such a toxic perspective. Somewhere in our evolution we have been led to believe that busy is good.

Everything in modern society is set up for speed and efficiency and if you don't have at least five programs open on your computer at any one time then you're a slacker! But just because you are busy, does not mean you will make money. You have to be busy at the tasks that produce money. Everything else is just fluff and bluster!

Tony also attended one of my seminars on making more money in business. His priorities were Creativity and Productivity—in that order. Again, money was nowhere to be seen. Surprise surprise, he was incredibly creative and his workload was amazing but he consistently found it hard to make money from his efforts.

John W. Gardner once said, 'All of us celebrate our values in our behavior.' I would take that a step further and say, 'All of us celebrate our values in our results!'

What happens if someone only wants money? They don't usually make it. To make money, money needs to be high on the list—plus some additional Success Drivers! If money's important but you're more interested in pursuing excellence and building an empire, then you will probably end up with all three!

Let's take Cathy as an example because a lot of people can relate to her. She has a job and is very good at it. She's diligent and hard-working, is of above-average intelligence, and committed to being successful. She has been to several wealth-creation seminars, in particular real estate investment seminars, all of which provided information that could have transformed her fortunes. Yet she still makes less than $50,000 a year and only has one real estate investment, which isn't performing very well. The bottom line is she THINKS she wants more money. So much so that she's started to feel desperate and buys lottery tickets in the hope she might pull off the big one. If you asked her, she would say money is high on the list. And on the surface that would seem to be the case.

The truth is very different. On the Success Drivers, Praise scored number one, Satisfaction of a Job Well Done was number two and number three was Competition. What was really driving her was that she wanted to be the most successful person in her company so the boss would praise her for a job well done. To her shock, money was not even in her top five. Interestingly enough, Cathy met every one of her top three drivers.

An Angry Young Man...

At the other end of the spectrum is a very angry young man I recently met. Let's call him Robert. Robert doesn't want to help anyone; he just wants to make a lot of money so he does not have to work. He doesn't want success or to improve himself, or to work for the money or take a risk, he just wants the money. He has a history of trouble and wants to win the lottery. Money is all he covets. Needless to say, he has none. You can't make money long-term unless you have another driver. It's a bit like what Zig Ziglar said, 'I can get whatever I want as long as I help other people get what they want.' Frank Bettger, who wrote the 1947 sales classic *How I Raised Myself From Failure to Success in Selling*, says something very similar: 'The quickest way to get what you want is to find out what other people want and help them get it.'

You need to work out what drives you, NOT what you think drives you or what you wish drove you. And the best way to do that is to look at your results. Look at the list and see what you are actually experiencing just now. Chances are, that will hold a clue to what you are driven by.

By consciously adding money to that mix, you can still meet your unconscious drivers; but if you also focus on money, you will be able to reap the rewards.

WORD TO THE WISE: if you want fame, praise, achievement or Drivers like becoming an empire builder, you might want to ask yourself if that is coming from thoughts like, 'I'm not okay' or 'I'm not good enough'. You might think that you can fill that hole in your soul by doing enough. However, I have met quite a few wealthy people who become raging workaholics, driven by the whip hand of, 'if you climb high enough, one day you will be okay.' There is another reason you might want to be careful about letting those kinds of Drivers run you—they can make you stoooopid. I knew a very successful person who specialized in large land subdivisions. They decided to build a 12-story development. They had absolutely no experience in this field, but were driven by the thought that if they did some huge project they would prove to everyone around them how awesome they were. It was awesome alright. Awesome failure. It cost them a fortune.

Personally, 1 like having Drivers like Contribution to Humanity and Abundance of Money at the top of the list, because you are less likely to make decisions based on your ego.

Can You Change? Can You Win?

"The only person you are destined to become is the person you decide to be."

—RALPH WALDO EMERSON

Can you change your Drivers? The good news is, yes, you can.

The minute you truly want something, your value system will change. Remember we talked about the SNAP POINT. It's the point you reach when things are really bad, or you've had enough. Whatever value system you have been running clearly doesn't work and you're getting yourself into deeper and deeper trouble. You crash and burn—and in that moment you change. Something inside you changes: what you value, what you want, what you're prepared to do, what you're not prepared to do—it all changes in an instant and a new future emerges.

Let's just take a minute to explore this a little more, because it's important. The reason reaching a snap point is so often the catalyst for change is because of emotion. Most people don't wake up one sunny day and decide to change things.

Usually they've reached a point where they've had enough. Often it is because they want a better life for their family, or someone else. One of the wonderful things about human nature is that we will invariably do more for someone we love than we will ever do for ourselves. I am confident that had I not had a wife and young daughter depending on me I would have been stuck in that mess for a lot longer.

I didn't realize it at the time, but the emotional pain I was in, as I sat in my scruffy kitchen, was enough to shake things up—and my Success Drivers changed in an instant.

And yours can too.

The snap point can also come at a very early age. I was skiing at a private ski resort with a guy whose net worth was in the nine-figure range. We had just descended through an untracked powder field and we were on our way back to the top. I asked him if there was a single moment when he decided to become rich.

A small smile creased his lips as he said one word: 'Absolutely!' I waited for him to continue. 'I was eight years old, on holidays with my parents, driving across England, through an area that was famous for Devonshire teas. My mother said, "Oh, let's stop and have a lovely Devonshire tea." My father just said four words, "We can't afford it." Sitting in the back of the car, I swore to myself that when I grew up, that was never going to happen to me.' If you don't have a snap point—the point where you decide to make it happen—it probably ain't going to happen.

Want to Never Work Again? Your Ultimate Outcome

Want to never work again? You have to ask yourself, 'What's in it for me?' It's great to have a purpose and help people—AND you can do this and help yourself too. They are NOT mutually exclusive. As we have said, the Architect is about the Big Picture—and part of that is where you want to be in the future. What I call your Ultimate Outcome—the goal you are aiming for in five to 10 years. Would you like to be financially free? If so, then maybe that needs to be your Ultimate Outcome.

If you want to get to a place where working is a choice and you're completely free, then the secret is in 'The Mango Tree'. Two people owned farms side by side. Mary grew mango trees, waited for the trees to bear fruit, then sold the mangos. Bill, next door, grew mango trees, but never waited for the trees to bear fruit. He just cut down the trees and sold the timber for firewood. You might think Bill is stooopid. However, I know people who make seven-figure incomes and spend the lot—that's like Bill; selling the mango trees for firewood is like living off the income you make. I also know people who make less than that, invest a big chunk of their income and live off the cashflow of their investments. That's like Mary, living off the mangos, using the income to create investments (which are like mangos) and not cutting down trees for firewood. In an ideal world we live off our investments and use our income to create more investments. Of course, it may take time to build up to this.

Here's a secret for you. When I first got into business, I was under the big misconception that a lot of people who looked rich, *were* rich. WRONG! Right clothes, right neighborhood, big staff, impressive premises—and they hardly had a bean to their name. They often have Success Drivers like recognition. I have met quite a few people who made a fortune and never put any of it into investments. One day, when the money stopped coming in from their business, they realized they had almost nothing except the spectacular house they lived in. They looked back on that decision with deep regret.

The One-Dimensional Architect

"Regret for the things we did can be tempered
by time; it is regret for the things that we
did not do that is inconsolable."
—SYDNEY J. HARRIS

I was in a cab heading to the airport. The driver was a man in his mid-fifties who had an aura of frustration and despair about him. He looked like a person who was nearing the end of a train ride and approaching the final station called regret.

We started chatting and I asked him about his day. As the conversation began to get a little deeper, he told me of a vision and a business venture he had nursed for many years. It was the one thing that would finally get him out from behind the steering wheel of a cab and into something fulfilling. I listened as he talked about what seemed to be the last thread of hope in his life.

Finally, I asked, 'What do you need to make it happen?'

He replied, 'I'm just waiting for my lucky break and someone to come along who can fund it.'

I got the feeling that he was hoping that one day a billionaire would climb in the back of his cab and just pull out a checkbook.

This taxi driver may have had a vision, but without having some of the other quintessential elements in balance, his dream remained dormant.

The person whose only developed element is the Architect needs the Achiever to make that vision happen. Otherwise, it will probably remain just that—a vision. Another word for a vision is an apparition, something that isn't real. To turn a vision into reality, rather than an apparition, you need the Achiever.

Without the Poet, the Architect runs the risk of jeopardizing relationships with family and friends by stumbling over their own arrogance. History is littered with the corpses of Architects who, puffed up by their own importance, made decisions that spelled their doom.

The Architect also needs the wisdom of the Sage to warn them of pitfalls on the way to fulfilling their vision. Many a fortune has been lost because someone denied their intuition in favor of an 'I can do anything' attitude.

How to Have All Five Elements

"The ancestor of every action is a thought."
—RALPH WALDO EMERSON

There are two ways to have all five elements in your life. You can have people around you that are strong in an element you are not. There are a lot of companies and partnerships where one person is an Achiever and the other partner is a Sage.

The other way is simply recognizing that these elements are a natural part of you, whether they are dormant or not. We all have them in varying degrees. The key is to use the information in this book to become more of what you already are. The first step is to intend it. Intention is the precursor of all things, and it is the most important and effective process to awaken all of the five elements. An idle interest is not going to be effective. As an Architect, you have to want to be a person who is committed to their unique vision, and commit yourself to becoming that person.

If you want to lift a book from a shelf, you first need to intend it. If you want to sail around the world you first need to intend it. If you want to go to the shop to buy a loaf of bread, you first need to intend it. Intention is seeing and feeling what you want and deciding that this will happen. It is a conscious choice to have what you want. The elements are already there inside you, but you have to *want* to awaken them. This intention has to come from a deep commitment.

The Achiever

*"I believe in challenges so great you know
they are going to stretch you."*
—Sir Edmund Hillary,
47 years after first ascending Everest

Achieving the Impossible

I woke up in despair. It had been five months. 'Keep going,' I
said to myself. 'I know you don't feel like it but keep going.'
Five months of going to an endless procession of doctors,
specialists, physios, healers and every expert under the sun. No
one knew the answer. I got used to their blank faces. No one
could tell me why I had been on crutches for five months and
had completely lost the ability to walk. One of my legs refused
to obey my mind. Some were starting to suggest I should just
give up my active sports life. There were people who wondered
if I would ever walk again. But I had a dream of a particular goal
I wanted to achieve in the future... and the raised eyebrows
from some people told me they thought that was completely
out of the question. When the drama first happened, the
doctors assured me it was a normal operation to replace the
ligament in my knee from a skiing accident. They told me I
would be up and around in a matter of weeks. Five months

later, I was still on crutches. The operation was a success, but all the muscles in my leg had mysteriously turned off.

The day things changed, I drove two hours to see a sports doctor who worked with elite athletes. I was assured he was the best and rarely saw outside patients. I crutched my way into the waiting room, aware I had lost so much strength. Simple tasks made me feel 100 years old. Despite a lot of rehab, my leg was shriveled and tiny. Still, I forced myself to be optimistic. The thought of giving up and never being able to ski or surf again drove me on.

The doctor across the desk had a wide forehead that suggested intelligence and warm, compassionate eyes. He examined me for a few minutes and then asked me a series of questions—questions that let me know he knew exactly what my symptoms were. *This is different.* Then he let me know what had happened. It was a very rare condition, but it had resulted in something that had turned off all the muscles in my leg. A spark of hope. I knew what I was dealing with. Three months later, with the help of a remarkable healer, I was off the crutches. After eight months, it gave me enormous pleasure to put the crutches in the back of the cupboard.

I knew I needed a goal to deal with the endless months and months of rehab in front of me. I already had a big one. There is a place in Colorado the locals call 'the extremes'. The locals there like to keep it a secret and try to avoid being on the tourist map. A lot of people rate it at as one of the most extreme lift-accessed ski terrains in North America. That became the goal. At first, the recovery was slow. One day as

I walked into the ocean I was hit by a tiny, one-foot wave. It knocked me over. I just didn't have any balance because my core strength had gone. Walking around supermarkets, I was on edge in case people accidentally bumped me. It gave me a real sense of compassion for the elderly and infirm and what they have to go through on a daily basis.

Early on in my program, I was lifting tiny little weights and struggling under the load. I graduated to working with one of the best strength and conditioning experts in the world and made progress. There were some arduous sessions pushing past the pain barrier, and yet I loved every minute of it. It felt sooo good to be active again. The strength returned and I kept seeing in my mind's eye a distant peak in Colorado. Even during the heat of summer, I could visualize the cold, the snow and the steep, wild terrain.

Fast-forward into the future... I catch a very early morning chairlift, looking at the towering, craggy peak of the mountain, framed in an icy blue sky. I ski up to the base of the next lift. A sign screams, 'WARNING: EXTREME TERRAIN EXPERTS ONLY'. I feel the butterflies in my stomach doing a conga dance. I jump onto the rope-pull lift and ascend into swirling snow and pine trees. I ski off the lift, my senses on full alert, around the bend in the early morning light, the sun hitting the tops of the emerald trees. As I pull to a stop, there is a breathless quiet. I stood on top of a vast, snow-white expanse where there was only one way to go—down. Falling was not an option. It was outrageously steep—off the charts—and went down for hundreds of meters. A wave of excitement and fear rippled through my body.

I looked down. 'This is what all the training is for,' I thought, and launched myself off the lip and into the abyss. I could feel my body wanting to lean backward—a false instinct to survive that was wrong and deadly; I would lose control of the skis. I ignored the survival instinct and forced my upper body to lean straight down the mountain. I hit the balance sweet spot and I could see the light dry powder snow pluming around me, coming up in giant sprays and the quiet 'shush, shush' as my skis came around beneath me. And then my mind went blank. I became lost in the moment, sailing down the mountain, not another soul in sight, the joy building and exploding as I let out a huge scream, 'Wooohooo!' I soaked in the moment and thanked God for the privilege of being in that wild place. I skied nearly all day and came home with a smile from ear to ear, glowing like a Christmas tree.

The Achiever's Blueprint

"A mighty flame followeth a tiny spark"
—Dante

The element associated with the Achiever is fire. It is the purifying fire that burns straight towards the goal. We often use the metaphor of fire when referring to the intention of the Achiever. Someone may be impassioned by a 'fire in the belly', or a 'burning desire'. When they are really committed to a mission, they might say, 'I'm on fire!' or 'I feel fired-up about this!' Achievers are tenacious, steadfast, determined and persistent. Like the element of fire, the Achiever burns its way to victory.

Achievers see the world as a place of challenge and an arena in which to test themselves. Enter the gladiators of the sports track and the business world. Anything that takes drive to be successful will see our Achievers crowding around trying to out-compete each other, whether it be at chess or ice hockey, or setting up an orphanage. There is nothing they like more than a challenge—except winning. They *love* that.

Achievers use the internal mechanism of competition to measure any action they are engaged in. If they are on a mission, they will evaluate how they are doing by comparing themselves to others or asking themselves if they are living up to their own standards. This evaluation spurs them on to their goal. It is their greatest blessing and their greatest curse. It is a blessing because this evaluation can lift them to higher and higher goals. But it can be a curse because sometimes it gives them no peace. As soon as they have arrived at their destination, they move on to the next goal.

The Achiever lives by a certain set of internal standards, and if they are not living up to these standards they will never be satisfied. Notice the word is *satisfied* rather than *happy*. Their happiness may be short-lived because their focus shifts to the next goal. Essentially, they are *outcome-driven*. They only see the achievement of the mission (which is why they need the balance of the Poet, as will be discussed later in this chapter). However, this drive and commitment to outcomes is essential in the pursuit of their ambitions.

Achievers are often one-directional in their approach to life: 'Get out of my way, I'm coming through.' There are a few people out there who wear the tire marks of an Achiever on a mission. Achievers believe in getting the job done above all else. Diplomacy comes later on their priority list. They want people around them who are doers. As a result, those who work or live with Achievers can find it difficult to live up to their high expectations.

Respect

Achievers have a unique value system. They primarily seek respect—from others and from themselves. The only way they can respect themselves is if they are living up to their own high standards. Many Achievers rank respect even more important than love. The reason for this is that Achievers are driven by the desire to constantly be at their edge. Their closest friends will be people they respect. In fact, the only way to ever become close to an Achiever is to first of all win their respect. A die-hard Achiever will evaluate people by what they have done or achieved. They may even overlook some serious character flaw in an individual if that person has achieved something momentous. Achievers abhor weakness and seek to live life on the edge.

Awakening Your Inner Fire

The first great quality of the Achiever is commitment.

"He that lives upon hope will die fasting."
—BENJAMIN FRANKLIN

What Was That Blur? That Was Your Life...

Four-thousand weeks! Your life span will be about 4,000 weeks. That's it! That's all you've got. Look back over last week. Did you spend that precious week wisely? Did you move toward the life you want? Or did you find yourself 'killing time'? Who in their right mind wants to 'kill time'? It's the most precious resource you have and it's the only one that is finite, so start appreciating that fact right now!

I am in a really privileged position in that I know that if I were to walk out my front door tomorrow and get run over by a bus, I honestly have no regrets.

The Achiever's game is really simple—don't die with any regrets. Or as Oliver Wendell Holmes Sr said, 'Everyone has music in them. Don't die with the music still in you. Whatever you want to do, do it right now.'

Ready to start? Here we go...

1. Mastering Commitment: The first step in maximizing your Achiever.

Commitment is that powerful state when all your energies are focused on a single issue. You are clear, on-target and alive. Commitment is the arrow-like force that emanates from deep within and drives your outcome to victory.

Commitment is the force that prevents you from becoming sidetracked. The Achiever, like the arrow, only knows one direction—straight towards the target. However, if that arrow comes from an archer who is distracted, it could land anywhere. Unwavering commitment is the rarefied domain of the Achiever.

69

It creates focus, drive and a fierce determined will. It is the Achiever's highest form of charisma. Commitment is the 'procrastination killer'. However, there are four steps on the ladder of commitment.

Level 1. Interested

There are four levels of commitment. Level one is 'interested'. If someone is only 'interested' in making more money from their business, then it rarely ever happens—it's just an interest.

Many years ago I was asked to be a guest speaker at a wealth creation program. I entered the room and everyone was hyped. The atmosphere was really positive and I could tell that everyone was excited about the possibility of being wealthy. But my radar detected the scent of BS—it didn't feel quite right to me.

As I came on stage I was welcomed by a sea of eager faces all intent on hearing whatever pearls of wisdom I would impart! I opened by asking the audience what the program was all about. They were halfway through the event and they were all pretty vocal. Several voices roared out, 'To create wealth and have financial independence.'

I said that I certainly couldn't argue with that and asked, 'So how many of you are committed to being financially independent?' Every hand in the room shot up. I could have easily moved on to the body of my presentation, and certainly that's what most presenters on wealth would have done. After all, it's all about giving the audience what they want. But I don't always agree with that. It's also about helping the audience understand what it is they really want and giving them real ways to achieve that. Not just hot air and promises.

Anyway, I repeated the question: 'So how many of you are committed to being financially independent?' Once more all the hands went up, this time even more vigorously than before. I kept repeating the question over and over and I think a few people started to wonder if I was mentally impaired! There were certainly plenty of puzzled faces in the crowd as people started to get agitated.

Finally, a big guy who was sitting at the back of the room rose to speak. He was literally a mountain of a man and commanded an incredible presence. The room hushed as he stood there. He looked directly at me and said, 'Brendan, I thought I was extremely committed but you've got me thinking. The truth is, what means more to me than anything is family. I've always wanted more money but I've never really committed to it.'

I looked at him and said, 'That's okay. At least now you know what you are committed to.' He discovered that being interested in financial independence is not the same as being committed to it. Every person in the room got a chance to speak. At the end of the night there were two people in that group who, beyond a shadow of a doubt, were committed to financial independence. Guess what? Those two were already financially independent.

Wanting to have something and hoping that one day you might be rich, will not make you rich. And there is absolutely nothing wrong if you decide not to be wealthy. That's your choice. What is torture though, is wanting it badly but not doing anything about it.

Level 2. External commitment

The next level of commitment is external commitment—commitment based not on what you really want, but the opinion of others.

I know businesspeople who swear they never operate from external commitment. One friend of mine had a company that employed 47 staff in a landmark building. This company won one of the most prestigious business awards in the country and was featured on television as a 'success story'. They certainly looked successful, yet they weren't making any real profit! One day the owner woke up and realized he was operating in the classic 'big is better' syndrome and his motivation was coming from 'looking like a success'. He took a giant axe to the business, regained his peace of mind and increased profitability.

I remember an experience of being caught in Level 2 when I started going out with my wife. On one of our first outings together, I picked her up in a Porsche that I owned at the time. As she was about to get in the car, I asked her if she would like to take the wheel. She looked at me with a mischievous smile, climbed into the driver's seat and proceeded to drive the car in a way that I had never seen before. I felt like I was in the car with a Grand Prix racer as she fanged around corners with a relaxed confidence. Later I found out that her father was a racing car driver and had shown her the ropes.

At the time, my male ego was twisted a little out of shape. A few nights later, I thought I better show her that I could drive like a rally driver. Normally when I drive, I am a bit of a cruiser. Cars for me have always been vehicles to get from point A to B. On this particular night, however, I looked like I was auditioning for a James Bond movie. I came around one particular corner well within the speed limit but definitely over-steering. I suddenly realized I wasn't going to make it no matter how cool I looked. I ended up putting a dent in my ego and the car. Essentially, I was committing to a level of driving that was based not on my own expectations but on what I thought someone else expected of me. In fact, in this case my future wife had no expectations at all. It was all my imagination.

It's the same in life and business. People commit to some ideal of what success should look like, based on others' opinions. The reality is that most people are too wrapped up in the drama of their own life to give a lot of attention to yours. External commitment is more potent than Level 1, being interested, but the next level is more powerful still.

Level 3. Internal commitment

You've figured out what you want. You are not concerned with how it looks to others. You're going to play your own game. You're now operating at Level 3—internal commitment.

When someone arrives at this level, they achieve a tremendous sense of freedom and independence. They decide their own journey and live by the rules they make up, not someone else's. They are not trying to live up to someone else's expectations. Instead, they are dancing to their own beat and setting their own goals.

Once you harness this internal commitment you become much more your own person. Moving from external commitment to internal commitment can be a bold and courageous step, because there is a fear that you will be disliked or abandoned. And yet to do anything else is to abandon yourself and your own dreams. This stage is powerful, yet the next stage is the apex.

Level 4. Totality

"The only way to discover the limits of the possible is to go beyond them into the impossible."
—ARTHUR C. CLARKE

The voice on the other end of the phone was hiding an edge of panic. It was just an average day when I got the call. I only knew the person on the other end of the phone by reputation. They were a serious player in the business world and they were in trouble. They had a 1,600-acre development that had been on the market for eight months and they hadn't made a single sale. They were staring down the barrel of a big, big loss and wanted to know if I could get them out of trouble.

I traveled out to the development and looked over the subdivision. The owner was a direct, no-nonsense sort of guy and I instantly liked him. He had handed the sales and marketing to another agent and so far, all they had produced was a big fat zero. When I studied the marketing that was being done by the current agent, I could see that they had gone to sleep on the job. To be honest, I felt upset he had been so badly let down. There were millions of dollars at stake and the managing agent had left him in a hole. I walked around the development, mulling the whole thing over in my mind. I became more and more certain this had enormous potential if handled in the right way. I weighed up the downside, then made a decision. I told him I could do it. From that moment I was ALL IN. Once I had made the decision, I was total. So many people, when they make a commitment, leave little escape hatches open in their mind: 'Yes, I am committed, but...' There were no 'buts' in my mind. Getting this project sold was my number one priority. I was 1,000% focused on making it happen. What happened? We sold the whole thing in six weeks without lowering the price. The owner was one happy guy. And he gave me an even bigger development to market, which we sold out too.

Over the years I have told this story quite a few times. The most commonly asked question is about the strategies we used. My answer is that the strategies were important but secondary to the commitment. Yes, all the copy, marketing and sales need to be spot on, but the strategies were only effective because the commitment was there in the first place. If you fully commit, the correct strategies will spring forth. They will naturally unfold.

What were the strategies? It was a rural subdivison, one hour and 15 minutes' commute to the city. All I did was focus all the marketing on attracting professional people who worked in the city and wanted to live on a rural subdivision with space. When I tell people that they often miss the point.

Yes, the strategies are important but come after being totally committed. In fact, when you are totally committed you will dream up ideas and have attention to detail that is beyond most people. I have given identical strategies to multiple people and the most committed person comes out in front.

The final stage on the commitment journey is totality. It is the realm where you go way beyond what you considered possible. Everything extraneous vanishes from your field of vision and nothing else matters but achieving your intention.

This is where corporations are born, great causes are supported and visions are realized. It's no longer about an individual and their goals—it's much bigger than that.

When you operate in a spirit of totality you command attention just by your very presence. There is something about people that are living full-tilt. It's almost magnetic and they invariably exude a rock-solid and unwavering focus. They emanate a sense of certainty.

The root of the word 'decide' actually means 'to cut off from'. A true decision cuts you off from any alternative route—it is a verbal commitment to that choice.

A lot of people say to me, 'I want to be successful and wealthy, but I don't know how to do it.' Sometimes you've got to put the cart before the horse. You've got to be committed before the horse can even show up. You've got to decide beyond any shadow of a doubt that you are going to achieve what you set out to achieve. It's a resolution set in stone. There can be no part of you that does not make the decision; you have to be congruent and fully aligned to that outcome.

And when you are, strange things will happen. As Goethe said, 'Whatever you can do, or dream you can, begin it. Boldness has genius, power, and magic in it.' And there really is magic in it. Strange forces that we still don't understand seem to conspire to help us achieve our deepest commitments. Buckminster Fuller, one of the great geniuses of the 20th century said something similar: 'The principles will be revealed upon the decision.'

The plan will form once the decision and commitment is made. If you want totality, then you need to master the two steps to having it...

Two Steps to Totality

Step 1: 100% attention

When I first met Ava, she was uncertain about what she wanted to do. She seemed torn between a multitude of outcomes. She talked a lot about the obstacles that confronted her in her business. We got her focused on exactly what she wanted to achieve and she changed—wow did she change. She became 'scary focused'. Don't misunderstand that term. Ava is one of the loveliest people you will meet, but there are a few people who get scared of her because she knows what she wants and is ALL IN.

There are two steps in achieving totality. The first is to summon all your attention. Let's imagine that your attention or focus was divided into units, which I will call 'attention units'. Say the total number of these units is 100, which is your total capacity for focus and attention. If you are engaged in a project, the first step is to bring all of your 100 units of attention into the project.

Great entrepreneurs have what I call 'sustained focus'. They have the ability to bring all their attention units into play and stay in that state for an extended period. It is actually very rare. Most people only bring a part of their focus into play and so are never fully 'there'.

Step 2: Closing Back Doors

The second step to achieving totality is to eliminate your back doors. A back door is a thought or action that sabotages your intended outcome. It is an escape hatch that you consciously or unconsciously know runs counter to what you want. When you commit to something and remove the back doors, you make an irrevocable decision. It is a goal from which you cannot escape.

Let's say you have a goal to make more money. At the same time, you are not prepared to take any risks, or you worry what people will think of you if do make more money. Worrying about what others think and being unwilling to take risks are two back doors that stop you really going for your intended outcome. Imagine someone saying to you, 'I'd like to be rich as long as I don't have to work harder.' You could see straightaway that they were not really total in their commitment. They had left themselves a back door.

A good example of closing back doors can be seen in what I now call the '$50,000 ransom'. In one of my groups I had a high-achieving entrepreneur who stood up and confided that he had never really committed to getting in shape.

As he looked around the room he said, 'I am rich and I have been on a lot of weight-loss programs but none of them have ever really worked. This time I am going to lose all 28 kilos because if I don't lose it in the next six months, I will donate $50,000 to charity.'

There wasn't a sound in the room. Everybody knew he was 100% committed to his goal. In one fell swoop he eliminated his back doors. Every time he thought about going near the refrigerator, he reminded himself of what would happen to his bank balance. Needless to say, he completed his goal.

When you combine eliminating your back doors with bringing all of your attention to a project, you attain the totality of the Achiever.

2. Mastering Action: The second step in maximizing your Achiever

Ready, set, charge! Actually, forget the 'ready, set'. For the Achiever, it's just charge! Action is paradise to the Achiever. They love storming the ramparts of their latest mission. The first quality of the Achiever that we discussed is commitment. To master the second great quality of the Achiever, you need to become action-oriented.

How do you become more action-oriented? The answer lies in what I refer to as 'windows'.

Imagine you are playing a computer game. As you travel through the game, you have the ability to click on certain characters or locations. This allows you to open different windows that take you to entirely new and amazing worlds. Each window opens a new opportunity for fortune and glory.

Well, that is what life is. Life is like a 360-degree, virtual reality computer game. There are always countless windows or opportunities appearing in your life, and each one has the ability to take you on a whole new adventure. All you have to do is dive through the window. We have all experienced these moments. Perhaps your window came when you mustered up the courage to ask someone out on a date. This may have led to a new life direction.

We all have windows in our lives. It isn't about finding more windows, it is about being aware of the ones that are right in front of you. Achievers dive through them.

When a professional tennis player hits the ball, they are looking to place it in a very precise position. The fact that the ball is coming towards them forces them to take action. They have to take the best possible opportunity when hitting the ball back. Life is the same; it is always coming at you. What may seem like a chance encounter could be an amazing opportunity.

Sometimes a window will beckon you for ages, other times it is a matter of seconds. You never know how long a window is going to stay open. Life is always moving and eventually that window will close, or you will pass it by. The key to taking action is to develop a window-leaping mindset. Just start training yourself to grab opportunities that are right in front of you.

Mary Ellen Sheets was on her own with two teenage sons, no money and a rusted old pickup behind the house. She looked long and hard at the pickup and decided to act. She designed an ad promoting 'Two men and a truck'. Along with her sons, she put the old pickup into action and created a company by the same name. Her business grew into a vast transportation company with over 2,800 trucks and 350 locations. Mary Ellen Sheets was someone who recognized the old truck as representing a window she could jump through.

Often, people wait for their one big lucky break. The key to getting that one big break is to take all the small breaks that lead up to it. To seize your occasional big opportunity, you need to step through all the small windows first. This creates the mindset of the Achiever.

The more windows you dive through, the more seem to present themselves to you. It is important to get in motion and start taking even the smallest of opportunities.

Inertia is just a habit. You can make diving through windows a habit too. The more you learn to take risks and develop this habit, the more it becomes ingrained as a natural response.

WORD TO THE WISE: Research what is on the other side of the window – look before you leap. However, if you look too long, that window can close.

The Achiever's Toolkit

How to Become Action-Oriented

The Secret of Outcomes

When I was training myself to develop my Achiever I had a small sign next to my bed, adhered on the wall right near my pillow. It was the last thing I saw before I slept and the first thing I saw in the morning. There were only four words on that little sign.

Those four words referred to the desired outcome I wished to create that day in my business and life. For several months I measured all my tasks by those four words. If I was preparing to do something, I asked myself, 'What is my outcome?' It was amazing how many tasks were suddenly scrapped because I realized that I didn't need to do them. I would go to my office and every task would be measured by those four words. 'What is my outcome?'

I realized that in the realm of the Achiever there are only results. I didn't want to go to work to take up time, I wanted to produce. That was my desired outcome, to produce results. Suddenly I realized how many phone calls or tasks didn't need to be conducted, and how many extraneous endeavors I was pursuing that did not lead me to my outcome. My income rose and the hours I worked radically decreased.

I am convinced that many people work long hours simply because they think that they *should*, to mitigate their guilt. They think that unless they are putting in long hours, they aren't achieving anything. If your desired outcome is to get to the top of a mountain, you have two options. You can call a committee meeting, plan the route and the supplies you will need, talk to others who have climbed the mountain and start the journey. Or you could just helicopter to the top of the mountain. If you are very clear that your desired outcome is to get to the top of the mountain, then you will take the second option. If, however, your outcome is to feel busy and hardworking, then you will probably go with the first option.

To develop your Achiever, try this exercise. For one month, measure everything you do by asking yourself, 'What is my outcome?'

If you are going for a meeting ask the question, that way you will cut straight to the chase.

The same question is also invaluable when dealing with obstacles that come up in your life. If you are faced with a problem, rather than letting the problem control you and becoming obsessed with how bad things could get, look for an outcome you want, a solution, and stay focused on it.

If you try this exercise for a month, your whole life will develop another characteristic of the Achiever—efficiency.

BIG INCOME TIP: If you are wondering about what kind of outcomes you need to set to dramatically increase your income, then set Two Primary Tasks in your calendar. These are tasks that will directly increase your income or cashflow in the next 60 days. Focus on those first. This subject is so important that we will go into it later in the book.

The Achiever's Four Steps to Having Big Results

Some writers claim that if you visualize what you want, you can manifest your ideal life without having to do any work. Good luck with that!

There is a sequence to manifesting anything in your life—whether you want to make more money or anything you want to have. I remember one of the most profound moments of my life where I really witnessed this firsthand.

Annie and I married only four months after we started going out. When we started seeing each other, it was nice and friendly and then after about two months it became very romantic. I asked her to dinner at an upmarket hotel, which was the only restaurant in the city that did silver service. It really was impeccable service; we were dressed to the nines and it was a wonderful evening. About three-quarters of the way through the meal a thought flashed into my mind. I'm a great believer in following your gut instinct and your intuitions. Completely out of the blue came the message, 'You've got to ask her to marry you.' It was so strong and so powerful.

At first, I was surprised and thought, 'You can just move right back out of my brain!' All the logical reasons why this was a stupid idea came flooding in—apart from anything else, we had only been seeing each other for a couple of months! And yet the feeling was really strong. I excused myself and went to the bathroom. I'm not kidding—I stood in front of the mirror with my hands on the washbasin, looking into my own eyes going, 'Are you crazy?' I was actually saying this out loud, and thank God no one else was there! But I knew I had to act on it. I went back to sit down and Annie immediately noticed something was different too and said, 'Why do I feel like running out of the restaurant?' I asked her to marry me and she said yes. We both lit up like a beacon and we've been together ever since.

At the time, both of us thought that it had come out of the blue, but it hadn't—not when you consider the sequence that occurs when you translate an idea into a reality.

Our relationship started with a single isolated thought. When I first met Annie, I remember thinking she seemed very interesting. I could have just left it at that and gone on with my life, but I moved to step two, where that initial thought happened more frequently. I'd find myself thinking about Annie more often. After a few weeks or a month, I realized I was thinking of Annie a lot. How many people have done this when they fell in love? Pretty soon you go from a few isolated thoughts to what's called 'streaming'. And that's the point of no return—step three. I was thinking about Annie all the time. So, when we went out to dinner, manifestation was the logical next step. It really wasn't 'out of the blue' at all. And that's what you do with all the major decisions in your life.

First it starts with a single thought—perhaps you think one day that you'd like to own your own house. Pretty soon you start to think about that idea more and more. You start imagining what it would be like and what sort of furniture you would have and where you would like it to be. So, the single thought gets more substance and strength. All of a sudden you're streaming— it's no longer a single isolated thought, it's something else altogether. Streaming happens when we start thinking about something all the time. Next thing you know, you're looking at ads online, you're visiting open houses at the weekend. You're seeing real estate agents in the areas you like. Then you find one in your price range and bang! You're buying your own home.

Here are the four steps:

1. Single isolated thought
2. Multiple isolated thoughts
3. Streaming
4. Manifestation

The really big quantum leap happens when you hit step three, and this was the stage I was at when I went out with Annie to the restaurant.

Manifesting is really fast when you're streaming. It's like that single thought opens up a door in your mind—like Alice in Wonderland—and soon it grows and grows until the door is big enough for you to walk through.

And this is how you do everything. The problem is that most people get stuck at step one or two. They have the single isolated thought about how nice it would be to make more money from their business, but that's about it. Or perhaps they graduate to step two, where that thought appears every now and again, but it never leaps into the streaming phase where it almost becomes an obsession.

The Snap Point we talked about earlier is usually the catalyst for someone to move from step two to streaming, and that's when things really start to change. 'Wouldn't it be nice to...' becomes, 'I've got to make more money.' A lot of the people I see in my seminars are already streaming because they are scanning the environment for anything that can get them closer to their goal. Everything about them is aligned to that vision and they are therefore pulling in the experiences, people, training and contacts that they need to make their dream a reality.

It is true that all of the major decisions in your life have followed these four steps. You fell in love this way. You bought your first house this way. You bought a car that you love this way. How many people have gone on the dream holiday after going through that process? First of all, somebody told you about Austria, for example. Wow, they've got these castles and you can drink coffee on the river and then pretty soon you're going, 'Wow, that would be pretty cool.' Then you go to step two and soon after that all you're thinking about is castles on the river. You're streaming.

WORD TO THE WISE: This also works on 'the dark side of the force'. This is how people get into drug addictions and alcoholism. 'I'll have a drink' turns into a regular drink, turns into, 'I have to have a drink' and you're streaming. Unfortunately, you're also an alcoholic! Same with drugs! This is the same process that people go through when they have affairs. They are in a marriage but notice someone else. Soon that's all they notice and once they are streaming it's a small step to cheating.

Steps one to four are how to create all the big positive things in your life and all the big disasters! You can stream negatively, or you can stream positively. Both are equally effective in bringing about what it is you're focused on. My advice, therefore, is to be very particular about what it is that you progress into the streaming phase. Here is a classic example of how one of my clients, a young man, turned around his life by using this principle.

When he first started working with me, I was able to show him a number of direct response marketing techniques that catapulted the income of his computer repair business.

However, after a year his income had radically dropped. Interviewing him, I found that he was spending a lot of time with a crowd that liked to party and drink a lot. His focus had completely changed. He was no longer streaming on wealth and success; all his focus was now on partying. As a result, a lot of the cash-generating strategies we had implemented were not being applied.

When he redirected his focus, the money started to come in once more.

Turning the Tough Road Into the Easy Road

"Two roads diverged in a wood, and I—
I took the one less traveled by,
And that has made all the difference."
—ROBERT FROST

The Achiever believes there are only two roads in life. Road one, the tough road, is the path of discipline and persistence.

Road two, the easy road, is the path of procrastination and distraction. An Achiever knows what few do: the tough road is the easy road and the easy road is the hard road.

If you have a project that needs to be accomplished in three weeks and you put it off to the last minute, you take the easy road. However, the ironic thing is that it eventually turns into the tough road when you start feeling stressed and working overtime to complete the project by the deadline. If you discipline yourself and start the project early, it may feel like you are taking the tough road, but this eventually leads to the easy road.

IMPORTANT: having trained thousands of business owners and entrepreneurs, the vast majority takes the easy road. When I go through the tasks they do each day, they often tend to put off the one thing they dread—the thing they find the most confrontational. The tough road is often doing the tasks that make you money. The only person capable of giving you money is a client or customer. The only way you can attract these people is marketing. Yet entrepreneurs will focus on everything except this. Ask the average business owner what they did in their day, and marketing comes in way down the priority list—they take the easy road, and the easy road turns into the tough road when they don't have enough cashflow. I am certainly not the first person to do this, but one time I asked a group, 'What kind of business are you in?' One person shouted, 'I run a law firm.' Someone else said, 'I am a consultant'; another yelled, 'I run a plumbing business.' Finally, after a long time, someone yelled out the correct answer, 'I am in the marketing business.' No matter what business you are in, you are in the marketing business. Unfortunately, what most people do when they want to make more money is try to increase their skill or their systems. While this is vital, the real key is to market your service, or product.

FREE – Do You Want Stacks of Low-Cost Marketing Strategies & Ideas That Can Create a Big Financial Breakthrough? Avoid losing thousands of dollars in wasted marketing efforts.

These little-known strategies are free at EpicVideoGift.com

The easy road/tough road also applies to your overall life. If you don't go for your dreams, you often take the easy road. Eventually though, the easy road turns into the tough road. I often hear elderly people say it is not the mistakes in their life they regret, it is the opportunities and dreams they never went for.

It often applies to our health too. Let's say you eat a ton of junk food mixed with gallons of coffee and alcohol, combined with the athletic prowess of Homer Simpson. Newton said, 'For every action there is an equal and opposite reaction.' That old easy road slowly turns into the hard road. The body just doesn't seem to have the get-up-and-go like it used to, and you start developing aches and pains.

Now, let's say one morning you wake up and your Achiever grabs you by the throat and says, 'Enough is enough, you're getting in shape!' At first it might be tough, changing your diet, eating healthy foods, puffing around the block and going to that yoga class. Gradually though, you start to feel better, your energy picks up and you're looking and feeling great. If you stay with it long enough, the good diet and exercise become a habit and something you enjoy. Voila! The tough road becomes the easy road. The Achiever takes the tough road because they know it will turn into the easy road. The Achiever understands that the tough road is overcoming obstacles, which leads us to a crucial concept—making mistakes...

Overcoming Obstacles

> *"Obstacles are those frightful things you see when you take your eyes off your goals."*
> —HENRY FORD

Have I made mistakes? OMG—of course! Try the time I got into a partnership with a guy who ran off with a big chunk of money. He had spent an extraordinary amount of time planning the move, while telling me in the months beforehand how much honesty and integrity meant to him. Lesson: listen to your gut, not just what they say. It is important to realize that you are always going to make mistakes. There will always be setbacks. It is how quickly you recognize and correct those mistakes that makes the difference.

If you have ever sailed a boat, you would know you are always correcting course. You cannot set a course and stay on it. You must allow for the tides, wind shifts and other factors. You may be heading for your goal, which you can see straight ahead. However, you will rarely get there by traveling in a straight line. That is the life of an entrepreneur. Occasionally something goes exactly to plan, just as the wind may blow you straight on course. Most of the time, however, you need to keep adjusting the course to get what you want. I often laugh when someone does up a business plan and thinks it will go exactly like the plan!

If you want to achieve great things, the key is to develop a mindset that picks you up off the floor after a setback as quickly as possible. What makes this easier is knowing and accepting that these setbacks are simply challenges. Life will constantly present you with challenges.

The Achiever has a very simple outlook on life that can be boiled down to a simple directive: 'Want something? Go get it.' To 'get it', the Achiever has a formula for success.

The Achiever's Formula for Success

1. Make a commitment
2. Take action
3. Deal with setbacks
4. Re-commit
5. Take action

You make a commitment, take action, deal with any problems you may run into, pick yourself up, recommit and start all over again. The key is to persevere, to just keep going. The

Beatles were rejected by a number of recording studios before they were finally picked up. Imagine if they had given up. The story of John Kennedy Toole is both sad and tragic. As a writer he suffered a lot of rejections for his novel *A Confederacy of Dunces*. He became so disillusioned by rejection that at 31 he took his own life. Years later his mother found the manuscript and sent it to publishers. Some of these publishers were ones that had already rejected him. The novel went on to become published and win a posthumous Pulitzer Prize for Fiction. *Eat, Pray, Love* was rejected for years, but Elizabeth Gilbert never gave up and it went on to become a huge success.

Success is rarely an overnight phenomenon. The key is to embrace challenges and setbacks as a natural part of life. Wanting life to be perfect and free of challenges is not only unrealistic, but also creates inner tension and discontent.

Someone who is a full-tilt Achiever knows that life will always be challenging. It is this knowledge that takes the sting out of setbacks. This understanding creates a tremendous freedom because you no longer see challenges as bad or horrible—you perceive them as the natural order of life. Once you know this, life becomes an extraordinary adventure.

Most people see their life as a series of benefits and inconveniences. An entrepreneur sees life as a challenge. A lot of the pain that humans experience is often created by trying to avoid a problem. Have you ever noticed that calamities are often easier to deal with than the apprehension about them occurring? These experiences are designed to help us grow. I get a lot of starry-eyed 'wannapreneurs' who think that when they get their venture up and running and they have millions, then there will be no more problems. HA! Until the day you check out, you will face challenges. If you can fully accept this fact, you will experience a momentous shift in the way you feel and perceive life. Try saying to yourself with excitement and conviction, 'From here on in, life will present me with challenges.' The Achiever embraces this viewpoint and draws strength from it.

Traits that Self-Sabotage

The One-Dimensional Achiever

If your only developed aspect is the Achiever, you can fall prey to becoming stuck in a rut. You may only see the 'straight ahead and charge' approach, not realizing there might be numerous options to get what you want. This can lead to exhaustion and to overriding your intuition.

If your only developed aspect is the Achiever, all you ever need to know about your shortcomings will be revealed in observing a fly.

Have you ever seen a fly trapped inside a room trying desperately to escape through a closed window? The little dude or dudette gets a full head of steam, and driven by the desired outcome of escape, batters their little noggin into the glass.

There is no doubt they are clear on their desired outcome—freedom.

Intention they have in abundance, but success? The scoreboard reads: Window—1,000; Fly—nil.

People whose only developed aspect is the Achiever can be as manic as the fly trying to escape. Just watch them when they first start a project. They can drive people around them to distraction.

You probably also know a few achievers who seem magnetized to the brick walls of life. They keep racing down the road, dressed in their red and blue Superwoman or Superman outfit, only to smash into an obstacle at high speed. Sure, they do have a few wins, as not all roads lead to brick walls, and they know about perseverance, but their red and blue outfits hide many bruises and scars.

Any fly (or human for that matter) with a highly developed Sage would perceive the glass. Their wisdom would tell them that this glass was impenetrable. The Sage is the one that says, 'Hey fly, I love your speed and intention but it would be a good idea to turn left now.' But this Achiever does not believe in inner voices—CRASH, again.

I've never talked to a fly in this state, but it looks to me that they are not having much fun. The Poet would say, 'Hey, let's chill out for a minute. We'll take a break, check out the sights and come back to the problem with some renewed energy.'

The Architect would say, 'Hey, wake up. Forget that window. That's not your path. Look over there—there's a window that's open.' Ever seen a fly do this? Just a few feet away there's an escape but they can't see it.

Of course, our Spirit would simply say, 'What's all the fuss? Surely you don't think you're really just a fly?'

95

A Sad Story...

Thinking about the fly reminds me of someone I met many years ago. I wouldn't have been more than 14 years old, but this one small encounter burned its way into my brain.

I was coming home from school when I walked down a long flight of stairs, into an underground train station. A gloomy yellow glow illuminated a tired group of shops near the platform. Walking through the stale, badly air-conditioned station, there was a burnt, gritty, metallic scent that seems prevalent in train stations around the world. I looked up at the board and could see it was another 10 minutes before my train, so I wandered into a shop to buy something to eat. I started chatting with the owner of this tiny shop, talking about my day. He was balding, somewhere in his forties, and a little stooped. After a while he said with an air of resignation and despair, 'Another day gone, another day closer to the grave.' He looked so tired when he said it, like the kind of fly who has realized he's going to die behind that window without ever getting through. This man was old before his time. He was a good person who was a one-dimensional Achiever. He worked really long and hard hours and was courteous to his customers, but he was doing something that produced very little love and a meager reward. He is not the only one either. I have met countless people who have bought themselves a job, they call a business. There is another way. Buying a job where there is no creativity, no opportunity to turn nothing into something, no potential for flair, no marketing ability—that is one looooong road. Don't be a fly.

The Stooopid Achiever

The brilliance of the Achiever is their ability to keep going and overcome all odds. It is a crucial element in getting to your goals. However, this one trait, while necessary, also has a serious downside. Robert Cialdini talks about a deep-rooted principle in people's psyche known as consistency. We have an innate need to remain consistent with previous decisions. I personally know one business owner who lost over $70 million by starting a business they had no experience in. The business was tanking year after year for 11 years, but they stayed the course even though some very smart people were telling them to bail out. They finally got out just before bankruptcy. They were driven by consistency and the principle of consistency can make you stooopid!

Say, for example, a business makes a strategic choice and runs full-tilt toward that choice. The more resources they throw at it, and the more time and energy they spend on it, the more committed to it they become, regardless of whether or not it's working. We need to be right, and rather than stop and admit we were wrong and change direction, we actually throw more weight behind it.

It's a crazy way to do things but it's a very strong driver and you need to understand how it plays out. Instead of backing off and changing tack, they spend increasing time justifying their original decisions. Some major businesses have done this with spectacular results.

For example, Motorola spent billions on a satellite phone system and, despite continued losses and countless analysts insisting they should shut it down, it took years and billions

97

in losses before they finally came to their senses. They were so hell-bent on remaining consistent with their original vision that they couldn't see that the market didn't exist. Or if they saw it, they didn't want to accept it.

Don't get too rigid, and take your ego out of play. Follow the money. Not the ego! It's the same with work. Only do work that creates an outcome you want. Getting a whole lot of stuff done is different to doing work that takes you to the outcome you want! I have met so many fiery Achievers who get through two tons of work a day and still never make any serious money or achieve the pinnacle of success. Some measure success as getting lots done—however you need to get the right things done to make it to the top.

A Walk On the Wild Side

I had a high-end group of very successful entrepreneurs who kept saying to me, 'Stretch us to the limit. Do something OUTRAGEOUS!' I smiled and thought, 'Be careful what you wish for.' I knew it had to be something that was outside the business sphere—they were already comfortable in that arena. So I took them at their word—I did something outrageous. And when I told them, the room went quiet... not a word.

We were scheduled to helicopter into one of the most beautiful and dangerous environments I have ever encountered: the glaciers and mountains of southern New Zealand. There the weather can change from sunshine to snowstorms in less than 20 minutes. The chopper pilots who fly there, and who have flown around the world, rank it as one of the most dangerous flying environments they have encountered. Apart from the deep snow and jagged mountains, there are glaciers with hundreds of crevasses. These crevasses are often well over a hundred feet deep and covered with a thin snow bridge. To the naked eye it looks like you are stepping onto flat snow. In reality, it is an invitation to the last six seconds of your life.

Day one of the expedition was the big eye-opener. Doctor Paul, a Himalayan mountaineer and remote medical rescue specialist, gathered everyone together. A wiry, fit guy with a humble demeanor, he never said a word, leaning up against one wall, waiting for everyone to settle.

The room was oozing bluster and bravado, these high achievers champing at the bit, ready to take on the mountains. Strewn around the room were backpacks, piles of ropes, crampons and other mountaineering gear. The place looked like an adventure sports store. Everyone had been briefed well before the event as to the hazardous nature of our little sojourn. We had all been in training for several months.

The doc patiently waited while one of the other guides explained that when the helicopters dropped us at the head of the glacier, we would be traveling in small teams to maximize safety. Everyone was psyched, ready to go, until our medico moved from his observation point on the wall and glanced at everyone. They could sense something was coming, then he said, 'I need to handle one important logistical requirement. In case anyone does end up at the bottom of a glacier, we need to find out if you want your body left there or brought back home.'

Talk about a reality check! The bravado vanished from the room, like early morning mist in the sunlight. The collective, unspoken conversation was, 'Oh my God, this is real.' The message was clear to each person. It was time to cross the commitment line.

The great paradox of commitment is that not being committed increases your risk. Not being committed, out there on the glacier, is an invitation to disaster for yourself and your team. Wavering in the middle of the road is much more dangerous than going to either side. There is nothing wrong with committing to *not* do something; for example, I take one look at ice hockey and say, 'No way.'

A few days later some of the members of the group talked about that moment of decision. Some realized that facing their mortality had forced them to re-evaluate their priorities. Others discovered in that one moment that they had been living as if life would go on forever, and it crystalized the importance of maxing out their existence.

The Poet

"Water is fluid, soft and yielding. But water will wear
away rock, which is rigid and cannot yield."

—Lao Tsu

I used to really suck at the Poet... and I paid a big price. Let
me wind back the clock...

The first big deal I ever got was 150 homes. The guy who built
them, let's call him Mr Crusty, was looking for someone to sell
them. He was fair, but as tough as they come. An old-school guy
with sparse red hair, his clipped, one-minute conversations passed
through a pair of parched, skinny lips that barely opened. No
facial expressions at all. You never knew what he was thinking. I
guess that was the plan. He had the air of someone who had been
scorched in a deal that had gone wrong. His basic position around
trust was, 'I will trust you after you have jumped through some very
big hoops.' So, before I got pole position in the deal there was a test.

He gave the first 50 homes to pretty much everyone in
town. He was going to see who came up with the best result
before he handed over the other 100 homes. There were over a
dozen different companies, and all their sales staff, desperately
trying to sell them. As the new kid in town I had to make a big
splash if I was going to grab this builder's attention and get
future deals. I didn't want to play in the shallow end of the

pool; I wanted to get into the big leagues of doing business with people like him and his connections.

If I didn't make a monster impression, I knew I would never see the rest of the homes. I set a giant goal. It wasn't good enough to just sell a bunch of them. I wanted to sell all of them. I revved myself up with my mantra, 'I'm going to do this if it kills me.' That was how I motivated myself back then: 'I'm going to do this if it kills me.' (I bet you are already seeing a flaw in my thinking.)

I studied every facet of the marketing. I left no stone unturned. I didn't sell 50. I sold 47 of them. Everyone was wondering, who the heck was this new guy? I got the builder's attention, and I got the rest of them for sale. It completely changed my business trajectory. Things took off and eventually I moved into an office in the middle of the city, hanging out with the heavyweights. What happened to Mr Crusty? Well, I guess I earned his trust, because one day he invited me to his home. I got the feeling this was a very rare occurrence.

So what's the problem, I hear you say? I got there, right? Sure, until one day a friend heard me say, in relation to another project, 'I'm going to do this if it kills me.' She looked at me and said, 'Do you really need to do that to yourself? Is it really necessary to smash yourself with that type of thought? I wonder if you could get there and be kind to yourself?'

Her comment hit me like a brick. It wasn't what I was doing, but how I was doing it. I was getting to the mountaintop but it sure wasn't a lot of fun. It was immensely satisfying (that's Achiever language), but as far as fun or joy? Not a whole lot of that, for sure. So, I dispensed with the flogging and started to have fun. And I still made it to the mountaintop. Go figure?

I see a lot of motivators advocating thrashing yourself with 100-hour weeks. I don't believe you need to do that. I learned how to get there and I took three months of vacation every year. Later in this section I will show you how I have taught thousands of people a method to earn more and work less. I discovered there is another way.

These days I also have a lot of fun...

When I was first starting in business, my early mentors were all very successful, but old-school. The work environment was professional and serious. When they left the office they had fun. One day I thought, 'Why can't you do both, have fun and be professional?'

One day I walked into the office with a hand over my mouth, bent over and moaning in pain. 'I think I have smashed my teeth,' I groaned. People looked up with deep concern. Then I took my hand off to reveal a set of fake, twisted teeth I had bought in the joke shop. Fortunately, everyone howled with laughter. Increasingly, when things get too serious I become the 'class clown' to lighten everyone up. You can do both, you know—be a very professional entrepreneur and have a blast along the way. The Poet is definitely about doing that and a lot more.

The Poet's Blueprint to Happiness

Unlike the fiery Achiever, the Poet, like water, is the great nourisher. Without water, a beautiful garden dries up, withers and eventually dies. We humans are the same. Without the watery Poet we become dry and lifeless. If you are overworked, burned out and are a fun-free zone, then you need an injection of the Poet.

To understand this element, watch a leaf in a bubbling stream. The leaf's journey down the stream does not resemble the straight flight of the Achiever. Whereas the energy of the Achiever is like an arrow flying through the air, the Poet, like the leaf, is more concerned with the process than the destination. The leaf is unpredictable in its travels, visiting one side of the bank before getting caught in a small eddy. Just when you think that it will be caught there forever, the water suddenly takes it on another adventure to the other shore. Water, like the stream, can wear down mountains of stress and tension. However, don't think for a minute that the Poet cannot help you get to the top. In the next section I am going to show you how one Poet took an impossible situation and made it extremely profitable.

Poets, like water, are fluid. They are spontaneous, loving and in a constant state of renewal. Poets experience beauty, being in the moment, romance and joy. They are optimistic, bubbly and hopeful. The Poet has their heart open to the world. The Achiever believes that happiness will come when they get to a goal; the Poet experiences happiness irrespective of where they are. When you have both your Achiever and your Poet fully awakened, you can head towards your goal and still enjoy the process.

Poets value love and harmony above all else. They abhor conflict and shrink from aggression. They are great romantics with wild flights of imagination, and in their ideal world everyone is happy and gets along. They long for surroundings that are joyful and serene. Their nature is one of great sensitivity. A kind word can lift them to the heights of inspiration and a harsh word can cut them to the quick. As a result, they are always on the lookout for environments that can soothe their soul and uplift their senses.

They love inspirational conversation, seeing it as a vehicle for connecting with other people. It is a way they can establish friendship and love. In business, the Poets are the networkers, creating relationships and influence. They have a huge circle of people in every sphere of life.

They will have five different windows open on their computer and three projects that they want to do, but they never seem to get to them. Being in the moment is their blessing and their curse. Someone who is only an Achiever will get to the goal, usually at an enormous cost to their family and those around them. However, if you think the Poet cannot make you extremely successful, read on.

Who Says Love Isn't Profitable?

It was close to impossible really. A reckless gambler used to taking ridiculous risks would never believe it could be done.

Sixty-six ski resorts across North America participate in a customer satisfaction review every year. This includes the big heavyweight ski resorts with their massive budgets. Basically, customers rank their level of satisfaction for every department in a ski resort. Competing amongst these goliaths is a dinky little ski resort in Colorado. I'd tell you the name but my local friends would kill me—they like the peace and quiet.

The results for this tiny-tot resort were pretty tragic really. I mean, how could they compete with such a small budget? However, one department came in number one, four years out of five. It was the ski hire department. The industry was completely baffled for a number of reasons—one of which was how this department looked to the eye.

As you walk into the ski hire shop and cast your eye around the paint-chipped walls and the battered counters, the first words that leap to mind are 'tired and grubby'. Looking over the selection of ski hire equipment that is available, the word 'limited' tumbles from your mouth. None of the huge selection of skis and boots available at the giant resorts were on offer. And the staff? If you were in a charitable mood, the word 'ragtag' would fit the bill. The big boss was always giving the department head flak about that. 'Can't you make them look more respectable?' And yet, they were winning and every other department was lagging way down the list.

You see, they had a secret sauce. A large raw-boned Aussie, Ian Hatchett, who moved to the little ski town decades ago. Few people knew he carried a past. He was an accountant who worked in the center of Sydney at one of the big prestigious firms. He was the golden-haired boy, earmarked for the top, until one day the thirst for a life of adventure became too much and he found a place where he could test himself amongst the extremes of the Colorado wilderness, and ascend the 8,000-metre peaks in the Himalayas.

One of the other department heads cornered Ian one day and asked, 'How in the hell are you winning every year and we are tanking? I mean, the store you work in sucks! They won't give you decent stock, they pay your staff rock-bottom wages—what's your secret?'

Ian looked at him and said one word. 'LOVE.' The other guy laughed, expecting Ian to laugh too, but Ian replied, 'No I am serious. That's the whole thing—love.' The guy looked at him completely bewildered.

The L word. Not cool to talk about that in business circles—I mean, it's flakey, right? No, it's not, but you have to know how to use it.

Every year, Ian assembled his team of young staff members. The kids idolized him. He was the same age as their parents and yet he didn't act like them. He was like an older brother, a coach and a mentor rolled into one. He was wildly passionate about helping people, and every year on day one of staff training he told the same story.

One year he was working in the shop a few days after Christmas. Like every ski resort across North America, it was pandemonium that morning. People rushing toward the slopes, ski lockers banging and everyone trying to outfit their families in near-Arctic conditions. Across the cacophony of noise, a voice that sounded like it had come from a cannon thundered in an angry Texan accent, 'What do you mean, you left your gloves in the condo?'

Listening to the story, the newcomers amongst Ian's ragtag kids looked bemused. And then he explained. 'This guy comes from Dallas. He works 50 weeks a year and has spent almost every dime he has to take his family of five on a ski trip, and now one of his children has left his gloves back at the condo. He is now faced with two options. Option A, he walks back to the bus stop in big heavy rental ski boots to get his child's ski gloves. He waits until the condo bus finally arrives and by the time he finally gets back it's lunchtime. Now he has to shell out a small fortune on ski resort prices for lunch. He takes option B—he buys another pair of gloves that are way more expensive than the ones he bought back at Dallas in the discount barn.'

Ian's crew, all without kids, begin to understand for the first time what it's like for the people who come into the shop. Ian drives the message home: 'Without these people, none of us would have jobs and be able to live in these amazing mountains. We have the ability to take them out of the grind of their day-to-day life and give them an extraordinary experience.'

Ian has everyone's attention. He revs them up even more: 'So here is what I want you to do: push the love out. That's your job, push the love out.' And that's what they did—they pushed the love out.

The constant gripe Ian got from the people on high was that his staff were not 'professional' enough. They wanted to make them stiffer. Ian's response was typical Ian. One of his staff went by the moniker of Doggy Dog. The higher-ups were always trying to get Doggy Dog to be less of a character: 'Why does he have to be so loud?' Ian just nodded, gave a wry smile and concocted a plan. One day, in the staff meeting, Ian looked sternly at the Dog and said, 'Give us your name tag.' Confused, he slowly unclipped the name tag with his real name, and handed it over. Ian reached into his pocket, pulled out a new name tag, then gave it to him. The new tag was emblazed with the name Doggy Dog. The staff all howled with delight. The big boss hated it.

When the families came back at the end of the day, Doggy Dog would look at one of the children and yell, 'Hey, Debbie, did you tear it up today?' Debbie would love it. The parents loved it even more, because they knew the people in the shop really cared. It wasn't an act. The most conservative Midwesterners loved the Dog.

Ian constantly reminded them, 'I want you to be yourselves. The love has to be real; it can't be an act. I don't want you to be fake about it.'

I asked him more about his philosophy. He said, 'The genesis of my philosophy is two things: living with consciousness and compassion. Compassion is the big love. My personal banner is, "push the love out".'

It's interesting to note one more very important thing. Ian was walking with his seven-year-old goddaughter one day. She was lamenting about how she doesn't have a superpower like Superwoman or Batman. Ian looked at her: 'But you do. Have you noticed how happy people are to see you? What you do is push the love out—that is your superpower.'

Love is a superpower. And if you use it without some strategy or act it can be mind-blowingly effective.

Fall in love with your customer or client, not your product or service. Most people are so enamored with their product they actually forget who's buying it. For example, I consulted a real estate company one time and I asked them how sales were. They said that they were not really selling anything except a particular block of units. I asked them more about these units and it turned out that everyone in the real estate office loved this development. It was right on the river and really represented where these guys wanted to live. My response to them was, 'Who cares what you like? It's all about what they like!' Their subconscious predisposition toward that particular development was translating into great sales, but why couldn't they get that excited about their other properties?

Their sheer passion for the apartment block was pulling in customers, but when they would show potential buyers a house in the 'burbs' they had no passion because it wasn't the kind of place where they wanted to live themselves. And so, people just weren't buying. I said to them, what you have to do is establish your customer's need. It's not about what you love, it's about what your customer loves!

However, it is very hard to love your customer or client if you have no regard for yourself. If you feel lousy about you, it's hard to feel love for them, and that's what we are going to cover right now.

Silencing the Scumbag Voice

One of the first steps in being happy and having a high regard for yourself is to stop being held ransom by your 'scumbag voice'— that voice in your head that denigrates you and constantly criticizes you. Here is a sample of some of its conversation: 'You, successful? Ha, not you, scumbag!' Or say it's a project you have been working on: 'It's not really great and for that matter you aren't either.' Or around meeting people you want to impress: 'You better put on a good act around everyone, or people will find out you aren't that great and reject you.'

I could give dozens of different examples, but it is just the part of you, that voice in your head, that pulls you down.

Do you have a scumbag voice? If you don't know, I'll save you some time—you do. We all have two voices: one that is positive and encouraging, and the other is the scumbag voice. It eats away at your self-confidence and happiness. It's the one that sniggers when you tell yourself you're going to be rich. It's the one that says, 'Not you, scumbag. Everybody else is going to make it, but not you.'

Don't be too concerned about this voice. Everyone has one. It's just a matter of learning how to turn the volume down or preferably hit the mute button.

NEWSFLASH: The scumbag voice is rarely understood in terms of how deep it will go to destroy your happiness and success. When most people talk about this 'inner critic' they just talk about how it denigrates you and tries to stop you achieving you dreams. It is FAR MORE INSIDIOUS than that! To get an idea of how it can destroy your happiness, let's see some of its varied strategies.

Imagine I run a podcast and that my guest today is The Scumbag Voice, talking about the seven miracles it can perform. Let's take a peek at the interview:

Brendan here, welcome to the podcast. Today we are interviewing your favorite enemy and mine—The Scumbag Voice. A pretty insidious little character, when you consider it has sabotaged millions of dreams. I will hand it over to The Scumbag Voice:

Hi, it's The Scumbag Voice here. I want to show you the seven miracles that I can perform.

1. The first miracle I can perform is to sabotage your success. I can do this with just a tiny invisible voice in your head. Pretty remarkable really. Imagine being able to destroy your life with just a voice—I would definitely call that a miracle. I get you to believe that if you are a scumbag then you never really deserve success. Miracle number one!

2. My second miracle is that I get you to become judgmental of others. The little secret I have is that people who judge themselves harshly will do the same to others. Getting people to judge others is a sure-fire way to destroy your happiness. Brilliant!

3. The third miracle I perform is I get you to judge people by feeling superior to them. If you think you are a scumbag and deny that, then you have to feel good about yourself in some way—why not judge the heck out of others? Guaranteed to destroy any meaningful connection to other people!

4. Or I do the exact opposite. I get you to feel inferior to others and become a complete failure. Quite amazing what I can do as a voice in your skull.

5. I am so brilliant that I can do the opposite of that too. I get you to become a workaholic and get to the top to prove you are okay. You are so driven to get there and finally achieve self-acceptance that you lose all joy in the moment, except the fleeting minute when you arrive, only to be consumed by the next project.

6. Here is one of my big miracles: never be who you really are and adopt inauthentic behavior. I mean, if you know you're a scumbag, the last thing you want to do is let anyone else know, right? Better to put on a false act—a guaranteed way to lose all personal sovereignty and be accepted. I also get you to never reveal you have a scumbag voice and put on a happy face. I mean, who would want to let others know who you really are—a scumbag? Then they would never love you.

7. And here is the biggest miracle of all: the funny thing is that I am not real. I can destroy your life with a voice in your head that isn't real. Who gives me power to accomplish all that? You do. And you also have the power to simply not listen. You have the power!

How You Overcome It

There are two ways you handle the scumbag voice. The first is you simply do not listen. If you had an enemy who followed you around all day telling you negative things about yourself, what would happen if you refused to listen? Eventually they would get bored and go pester someone else! And that is how you handle the scumbag voice—refuse to listen! Do not give it any energy!

Your scumbag voice is just a little voice inside your head. It's perfectly normal and you're not going nuts, so don't worry. But it's not helpful if you constantly listen to it.

Don't listen. Most people think that's too simple, but it is usually the simple things in life that make the biggest difference. If you continually ignored a schoolyard bully, he or she would eventually find someone else to annoy. Even if you have to pretend to ignore that person and remain poker-faced eventually, they'll get frustrated at not having any effect and go away. The scumbag voice is the same. Just hit an imaginary 'delete' button in your mind and get on with being successful. As you get more practiced at this you will be surprised to find that you hear it less and less, until eventually it's just a little murmur from your past.

The second way to overcome the scumbag voice is do the seven-day challenge. It only takes 90 seconds a day.

HERE IS MY CHALLENGE TO YOU: for the next seven days ask yourself three times a day, **'What did I do right today?'** Then you make a list. If you don't have a lot of time, make the list over 30 seconds in your mind, or better still write it down.

Really TAKE IN what you are doing 'right'. For the next seven days forget the scumbag voice or the part of you that thinks you are not performing. Sometimes we get so busy seeing what we are doing that isn't right or perfect, we forget to focus on what we are doing that is great. This is a fantastic way to increase your confidence and give you a healthy momentum to get to the top. Just 90 seconds a day. Simple!

Refining How You Motivate Yourself

WORD TO THE WISE: people think if they give up the scumbag voice then there will be nothing to spur them on to greater heights. Constant inner criticism is not a healthy or viable path to success. Imagine doing that to a child. By all means look at yourself and challenge yourself to greater heights, but constant judgment is just going to wear you down. A lot of people use their negative voice as a way of motivating themselves. This is okay in the beginning of your journey. I know in the beginning, I wanted to prove I was okay—show the scumbag voice was wrong, that I could make it. I also wanted to prove a lot of my schoolteachers wrong. Particularly the teacher who kept telling me I was useless and would never amount to anything. I used it as fuel. However, if you do that all your life, it comes at a cost. It is also coming from your ego—you are admitting you are flawed and trying to prove you aren't. You aren't flawed to begin with. It's like owning a Rolls Royce and everyone tells you it's a 30-year-old, beat-up clunker—you run around trying to prove them wrong and convince yourself in the process, and all the while you actually own a Rolls Royce! The truth is that who you really are is amazing. You don't have to prove it. Over time you can motivate yourself for other reasons. They could be: it's fun; or it's a fascinating game; or you want a particular outcome that gives you more freedom and helps other people at the same time. It is a far more elegant path than flogging yourself while you ascend the mountain.

Taming the Control Freak

A Journey to a New World

"To see a world in a grain of sand and a Heaven in a wildflower, hold infinity in the palm of your hand and eternity in an hour."
—WILLIAM BLAKE

'Let's face it Brendan, lately you've turned into a bit of a control freak.'

Looking at my wife, I smiled. 'Care to elaborate?' I knew she was going to elaborate anyway.

My wife Annie, who is the most patient, kind-hearted person I know, replied, 'Well, your seminar schedule is fixed a year in advance and I already know what kind of holidays we will be having. It will be an adventure surfing some remote island in Indonesia or charging down a ski run in Colorado. You never used to be this fixed. Don't you think it's time we do something different?'

I had a feeling she already knew what 'different' was. 'Watcha got in mind?'

'Okay, here is the deal. You let me organize an entire trip—it's somewhere in Europe. The catch is you won't know where we are going until you get to the airport. After you land in a city in Europe, you will never know where we are going next. I will be in total control. You are just the passenger and can offer no suggestions on where we are going.'

'Okay I'm in, let's do it.'

My wife, who was born in Finland, said, 'I'll show you the real Europe.'

I turned up at the airport, suitcase in hand, feeling tremendously excited. I didn't have a clue where we were going. Here I was a seasoned traveller, and it was as though I'd never been to an airport before. I felt like a kid and I couldn't stop smiling. I wondered what was in store for me. Annie was leading the way, when she began angling toward an airport counter. There was a buzz of people around us and I was craning my head, trying to see the small sign that would be our destination. Finally arriving at the counter I saw the sign above us—'Zurich'. I just stood there with a big grin on my face.

It was a couple of hours driving, after arriving in Zurich, when it really hit me. We had driven through some pretty countryside, but nothing prepared me for what came next. As the car came around a corner, there in front of me was a scene from a Tolkien fairy tale. I gasped in wonder and tears filled my eyes as I looked across the river to the striking old town of Bern. The 1,000-year-old town rose solidly up from the riverbank.

At its base, majestic ramparts, like a fortress, seemed to speak of another time. One minute, a modern world; the next, an ancient one. I hadn't expected it and was completely taken by surprise. No wonder the world is such a place of amazement to little children. It is still fresh and new.

We traveled on through winding mountainous roads and the clear sweet air of the Alps, where an endless vista of solitary peaks stretch out to the horizon, through tiny rural villages where farmers worked the land by hand, all the way to the opulence and wealth of the Riviera where diamonds and luxury cars competed for attention.

Every time we landed in a location, I had no idea where we were headed next. My urge to plan went out the window as all my attention was channeled into one day at a time. I remember looking out from the hotel in Monaco at the sleek white yachts on the still blue sea, feeling utterly carefree and at peace with the world.

We cruised on through the sun-drenched towns sandwiched between the azure waters of the Mediterranean and the rising green hills. The sensual holiday ambience of the coast was amazing. Every day the sky was cloudless.

We crossed the Italian border and arrived at an old fortress town situated on a craggy hill in Tuscany. I spent days inside the walled town, wandering through 800-year-old back alleys and laneways. I remember walking down one of these twisting darkened passageways finding the most exquisite detailed carving, hidden from prying eyes. I gazed at it wondering whom the forgotten artist was who had carved in such precise relief this hidden work of art. How many centuries ago had they toiled? Did this mark the wall of some once-noble family, now forgotten? If this carving had been on a building where I came from, where 'historic' is measured by a single century, it would have been one of the gems of the city. I was completely lost in the moment.

> *"He who can no longer pause to wonder and*
> *stand rapt in awe is as good as dead."*
> —ALBERT EINSTEIN

Perhaps you are wondering, 'What the heck has this got to do with being an entrepreneur?'

A lot, actually. I can't tell you how many people I know who struggle up the ladder, become multimillionaires and end up jaded and a little hard-boiled. Ever seen pictures of the top of Everest? It's beautiful but also bleak and inhospitable. The 'blast-through-brick-walls Achievers' bash their way to the top and find that the mountain peak provides great satisfaction, and a big burst of happiness, but it does not give an endless supply of joy or contentment. So, they find another peak and repeat the process and often the joy of life disappears.

You CAN HAVE BOTH. You can scale peaks without losing the buzz of life. I am also going to show you how the Poet will make you a far better and more successful entrepreneur.

The Poet's Toolkit

Free Up Some Time—Work Less!

This is incredibly important. The simple fact is that if you don't free up some time, it doesn't matter what I tell you in this book, you probably will not do it because you are rushed off your feet. And instead of fast-tracking your journey to wealth and success, all I'll succeed in doing is fast-tracking your journey to despondency. All you're going to get is a renewed sense of failure as you add even MORE things to your to-do list that you know will never get done! And that's not going to help anyone!

If you are already a business owner, I have little doubt that you are already stretched to breaking point. I know that you are the proverbial duck on water—calm on the outside and paddling furiously underneath. Or perhaps you've dispensed with the formalities and are paddling like a maniac on the outside too! Everyone, including you, knows you are drowning, so the idea of changing things or adding things is just too much to bear, so you will ignore the advice and struggle on as before. And I really don't want you to do that because I know that what is contained in this book could revolutionize your business and your life.

So the only way that you will even try this stuff is if you can recover some time to dedicate to it. And that's why this step is imperative to your success. You have to find some time to implement the rest.

So what should you focus on? You should make this your mantra: 'The most money, in the shortest amount of time, with the least amount of effort.' Write it down, stick it on a wall and look at it every day. Want to know a big secret? There is a reason I got to take three months holiday a year. I focused on two things: contribution and net profit. I hear so many business owners bragging about their turnover. Who cares? If your business has gross revenue of five million and you have five million in expenses—you got a big fat zero. When I say net profit here is what I mean—ACIP.

Actual Cash In Pocket.

An accountant will tell you that net profit contains future payments that are on the books, but in the real world, 'it ain't cash baby until it's in your pocket'. It needs to be ACIP. I don't necessarily mean the folding stuff, I just mean cash. And if you use this cash wisely to live an actual thing called LIFE, then you are going to have more time.

> *"We prefer businesses that drown in cash."*
> —WARREN BUFFET AND CHARLIE MUNGER

How do you achieve this wondrous state? For me it meant focusing most of my time at the Nexus Point...

I am about to give you a HUGE tip.

The Nexus Point is a secret only known to a small percentage of people AND they are the ones that make the money. If you really grasp this point, your life can radically change.

The Nexus Point is simply the point where the business actually makes money. It is the point when you or your agent (website, social media, salesperson, advertising, and so on) meets a client or customer. The ONLY person that can give you money is a client or a customer. If we divide a business up into essential categories like accounting, paperwork, team meetings, admin and so on, and really put them under the microscope, we will find that none of them create a Nexus Point opportunity. None of them create ACIP. Yeah sure, planning, meetings and administration are all essential ingredients in a successful business, but none of these endeavors create a Nexus Point opportunity—the opportunity to make money.

There are only two areas that create a Nexus Point. Sales and marketing. These are the only areas that create ACIP, because they create and MAINTAIN a client. And a client or customer is the only person that can give you money!

Now, a lot of people think that marketing is advertising. Marketing is infinitely more than advertising. Advertising is just a tiny component of the marketing mix.

Most of the marketing that people have seen is 'image' or 'institutional marketing'. However, the marketing that I have spent decades researching is direct response marketing. Direct response marketing is about low-cost, measurable strategies that make the 'cash register' ring in the next few days or weeks. Image marketing is about promoting the brand of the business. Image marketing is costly, lengthy and does not necessarily make you money immediately. I am not opposed to it, but only if it comes as a consequence of direct response marketing. Institutional marketing can work for recognized brands, however if you are a start-up, I believe it is best to do things that bring in cash. Many businesses have used this approach and built the brand as a natural result of that process.

Having trained tens of thousands of people on three continents and worked with countless business owners, less than 5% focused on the Nexus Point prior to working with me. Most are focused on work that does not create a direct profitable outcome.

One of the keys to making money, therefore, is to get more of your time back from unproductive areas so you can focus on the Nexus Point, make more money, and have more time off as well! If you focus on the Nexus Point, then you need to outsource or get others to do the non-Nexus Point work. You just need to monitor that they are doing a great job.

The Phenomenal Power of Income Time vs Busy Time

In my seminars I get people to list busy time (tasks that do not directly produce ACIP) and income time (ACIP tasks). They rank how much of their day is spent in which area. There is always a strange silence that comes over the room as the penny drops. After all, it's common sense. When you understand the Nexus Point, then it makes sense that the only time you will make money is when you are spending time working on aspects of that Nexus Point. Essentially, you only make money when you are engaged in income time. Everything else is busy time.

Every time I ask people to apportion their week based on these two types of work, almost everyone in the room realizes that they spend about 90% of their time in busy time. You don't make money in busy time. You might be doing things that are important and necessary for your business, but you don't make money. As Goethe reminds us, 'Things that matter most, should never be at the mercy of things that matter least.' So, the first thing you need to do is highlight for yourself how much time you spend on busy time versus income time, so you can recover some time.

TRY THIS: Write down all your activities under both categories then calculate the percentage of time you spend in busy time and income time. Most people who do this have a profound wake-up call.

Now, while many busy time tasks are vital, there are some that could be a waste of time. Scrolling through the web, getting distracted from what your Ultimate Outcome is—the goal you are working toward in five to 10 years—can only lead you further away.

I think for most people, the reason they don't commit themselves to more income time is that this is where the 'Fear Zone' is. The Fear Zone, in relation to income time, is that it is confronting. In the beginning it is confronting to put yourself out there, do the things that make money, write great marketing copy, and be proactive. People avoid the Fear Zone. They stay stuck in the Safe Zone. The Safe Zone is sitting on the sidelines; but no one ever played a game of football, tennis or hockey sitting on the sidelines. You have to cross that thin white stripe that separates the sideline from the playing field. And that is what terrifies people. It's the thought of just putting one foot over the line.

Once you take that first step, it is usually so much easier. That's where the Achiever comes in. It's that first step, like having to make a sales call, or putting yourself out there on social media, that propels you into income time. For some people it's scary. But the funny thing is that once you take the first step, there is often a wave of relief and an incredible feeling that you are accomplishing something. As Lao Tzu said, 'The journey of a thousand miles begins with a single step.'

Do You Really Deserve It? I Mean Really...

If I had a donut for every person who lost a lot of money and later said that when they searched their heart of hearts, they felt they never deserved the money in the first place, well, I would weigh a lot more than I do now.

Having worked with countless people, guess what is one of the biggest stumbling blocks to wealth, delegating unwanted tasks and most importantly, having an awesome life? It is the ability at a core mental and emotional level to truly feel like you deserve it with every fiber of your being. Oh, I know everyone wants it, but feeling like you deserve it... well that's another story.

Think this is not relevant to most people? That's a mistake. Here is a simple example that huge numbers of people struggle with—taking time off. So many people feel guilty about sitting around doing a whole lot of nothin'. Yet part of being a Poet is having the time to actually have a life instead of being a human doing! It's also feeling at that deep level that you deserve an extraordinary life. That you deserve it! Of course, you have to do something about it and that's the realm of the Achiever.

However, there are train-loads of Achievers (not on the train by the way, but pushing it uphill), who never have that life. Or if they do, it is only when they are exhausted; then because of their nature, they keep flogging themselves onward and upward. The Poet has a secret. They are awesome at nurturing themselves. Go to a spa and there are countless Poets having massages, acupuncture sessions or lolling about in the hot tub, because they simply know they deserve it. There are Achievers there too, but usually as a reward for hammering a big goal, or it is just part of their recovery process before they are out the door to compete with the world.

Interested in getting there more easily? Well, stay tuned while we peel back the curtain...

Four Steps to Deserve That Awesome Life

There are four steps to mastering a high level of deserving. I call this the Deserving Circle. A circle where each step feeds into the other steps.

Step 1. Contribution. The ability to give. Giving is a three-part deal. We talked about 'pushing the love out'. The second part is giving your time and your money to people who are less fortunate, and the third is a strategy I use that is commonly known as 'under-promise and over-deliver'. During a difficult time when everyone was in pandemic lockdown, I literally tripled the amount of information I originally promised to my mentor group. That is to under-promise and over-deliver. By making a contribution and giving out to the world, you kick start momentum on the Deserving Circle. People want to get rich quick without giving first. Or they want to become big without offering some great service or product. It's probably not going to happen.

Step 2. Asking. There is an old saying, 'There is no harm in asking.' If you don't ask, then the answer is no. If you have a great product or service, you have to ask for the sale—that is sales and marketing. It's the same with getting support from people who will help you get to where you want to go. You have to ask!

Step 3. Embracing. You've asked for what you want, now you need to completely embrace and totally receive what people are going to give you. You have to believe that you are worthy of receiving support from the world. The Achiever, who believes in competition, goes out, puts in huge effort and takes the prize—that is a valid strategy. However, the Poet believes the world is a benevolent place and wants to use cooperation with others to get to the prize. The ability to receive what others and the world are giving you at a very deep level makes the journey easier. When you truly embrace that you deserve to be supported, you have moved to the next and final part of the circle. Embracing and deserving also include the ability to self-nurture. To have massages, walk in nature and participate in any activity that rejuvenates you.

Step 4. Gratitude. Gratitude reinforces every step in the circle. It expands you to higher possibilities. Gratitude is one of the gateways to the Poet. By using gratitude, your level of happiness can soar and you can open yourself to a more expanded state.

If you had a child that was always griping about everything they had, would you feel like giving them more? On the other hand, if a child thanked you and was grateful for what they had received, it would probably open your heart to give even more.

I urge you to try the following exercise for 10 days and observe the difference it makes. It only takes five minutes and has the power to change the way you view your whole existence. It not only changes your perspective but also opens the floodgates for more to enter your life.

I find this exercise is best done when you first wake up or just before you go to bed at night. Buy a small notebook or journal and set aside five minutes every day. If you are particularly committed, try five minutes in the morning and five minutes in the evening.

Start a fresh page every session and write, 'Today I give gratitude for...' across the top of the page. Then let the pen write.

There are two important aspects to this exercise. The first is to keep the pen moving. If nothing comes to you then just slowly make lines across the page. This way you will access a deeper part of yourself. Your words will be less contrived. Just wait until something pops into your brain—words or feelings. You might write, 'Today I give gratitude for my partner, my children.' Another day, 'My friends, my job, that great conversation I had with Mary.' If it has been a really rough day and the only thing you can honestly write is 'Today I give gratitude that the day is over,' then start with that.

The second important thing is to write down some things for which you are grateful to yourself. You might write, 'I'm grateful for my patience' or, 'I'm grateful for not putting up with being taken for granted' or, 'My compassion' and so on. It is important to see yourself in a good light. This part of the process is vital. It allows you to be less judgmental and more appreciative of yourself.

I have often asked people, 'Who treats you worse, your worst enemy or yourself?' Some people reply that they couldn't imagine a worse enemy than themselves. See if you can stretch yourself into recognizing your good qualities and good points.

As you complete the exercise, write two simple words: 'Thank you'. See if you can genuinely mean it. Gratitude is a feeling or an energy rather than lip service. When you are genuinely grateful, you open the floodgates for even more to enter your life. It truly is an awesome power. Not only that, your entire thinking changes. You start to see so-called negative experiences as learning experiences; they lose their sharp edges. The result is, you experience more equanimity and contentment in your life.

I can hear some people saying, 'Oh great, if I get run over by a car on the day my insurance lapses, you want me to be grateful? You've gotta be kidding!'

Start off small and write things that are true for you. If you are not grateful for something, don't write it down. Remember to be authentic.

Chasing the Elusive Bird of Happiness

> *"If you are distressed by anything external, the pain is not due to the thing itself, but to your estimate of it; and this you have the power to revoke at any moment."*
> —MARCUS AURELIUS

129

I know multimillionaires who are very happy. I also know people who never seem to be satisfied, no matter how much they have. There is a litany of rock stars and famous people who had everything, but traded it all for the needle or bottle.

There is nothing wrong with having money and beautiful things in life. The Poet loves to surround themselves with beauty. However, you delude yourself when you say that you will only be happy when you have those things. You can be happy right now. It is a choice. In fact, you can be happy with very little, as I discovered when I visited a very remote island in the Indonesian archipelago with a group of friends.

We had been traveling for days over some of the thousands of islands that make up Indonesia. We were 'island hopping'. We would drive all the way across one island, then put the cars on the archaic ferries, and move on to the next port. Each time we headed further away from civilization. Finally, we arrived at an island for which no tourist brochures existed and where travelers almost never ventured.

There is something that takes place when I am far away from civilization. Being in the natural environment with people who have not been ensnared by the Western world allows me to remember what is really important in life. On the island, time moved very slowly.

We had been on the road all day. In reality, calling the pot-holed dustbowl a road is a massive exaggeration. Everyone was hanging on to whatever they could grab as the car lurched out of another giant pothole. The bush surrounded us on all sides like something out of the African plains.

Finally, I saw the village, a collection of thatch houses, up ahead. About the same time, the villagers heard the low pitch of the four-wheel drives. No one owned a car in this village, so they began to gather, curious as to who was visiting. We drove closer, and a call went out as they saw our faces. They were running towards the car, the shy ones in the back. God knows when they last saw people like us. Everyone mobbed the car, a sea of brilliant white teeth, set in happy brown faces. The kids are amazing. When you exit the car, they want to grab your hand.

Their innocence and playfulness automatically make you smile. They have no concept of adults who do nasty stuff. They are not like the kids in the West at all. You realize then that though they have nothing, they have everything. Does it sound like I am advocating poverty? Absolutely not. Because the villagers don't think they are poor. They have less than a lot of 'poor people' in our part of the world, yet something is different.

My friend Kim, a large wild man with a big heart, towered over the huge mob of kids. He pulled a balloon out from his pocket, put it to his mouth and blew. All the kids were astounded as they watched the balloon expand. They had never seen this trick before, or, for that matter, a balloon. He threw the inflated balloon toward them and they went wild, laughing and jabbering a hundred miles an hour. All the adults were in on this now as well. Everybody was laughing and playing, watching as red, blue and green balloons bounced from hand to hand. Their laughter was so natural, playful and infectious that we were laughing too.

As I looked around the village there were none of the conveniences, cell phones and screens that in our society we call necessities, yet these were some of the happiest people I had ever encountered. They genuinely cared for each other and were quick to share a smile. Their inner world was very rich.

It is worth keeping in mind that all of this joy in the village was over a bag of balloons that probably cost a dollar.

I have met so many people in our society who need a very large event in their outer world to produce a small shift of happiness in their inner world, such as those who believe that if only they had more money or got that promotion, they'd be happy.

If you are waiting for your external world to change before you can feel happy on the inside, you are giving your power away. Essentially you are saying, 'Hey, I'm not in command here. I am a leaf in the air being buffeted by the wind.'

If you say to yourself that you can only be happy with a certain set of circumstances, then you give your power to those circumstances. If someone believes they can only be happy when they have a private jet and a 10-bedroom house, then the jet and the house own them; the concept of the jet and the house contains the power. It is a subtle form of slavery and it is they who have enslaved themselves.

Very few people, whether rich or poor, really understand how to use money wisely. As I have said before, the only purpose to money is to 'get a life and give a life'. How many people really do that? I have friends who are rich who do have an amazing life, living on the edge. I also know a lot of wealthy people whose holidays are very sheltered and 'safe'. They stay in a narrow zone and fear to tread into the 'wild'. Seeing some of the wild places wakens the wildness inside us. It makes you ALIVE!

In terms of hotels or accommodation, I like to do no star or five-star. I have stayed in some of Europe's most famous hotels. However, I don't like the mediocre middle. Want to do no star? There are plenty of places out there that are still wild.

Traits that Self-Sabotage

The One-Dimensional Poet

The Poet seeks happiness. If you have ever met a 40-year-old whose only developed element is the Poet, you have probably noticed they are not all that happy. They are still smiling on the outside, but they're starting to look a little battered and disillusioned. A lot of their dreams and ideals have not eventuated. The life they thought was effortlessly going to fall in their lap just hasn't happened.

The strongest aspect of the one-dimensional Poet is the sense that they are insubstantial. You get the feeling that if you poked them in the chest your finger would go right through them. It is because they have not developed their Architect, an inner strength that comes from a core set of values and a mission in life. Those around them never fully know if these one-aspected Poets can be trusted or counted on in an emergency. Will they stick around or, like a butterfly, flit off somewhere else?

The one-dimensional Poet gets all excited about a new business venture, but pretty soon flits off on another tangent, never seeing things through. They are always looking for their 'big break'. Many relationships with a one-dimensional Poet are wonderful in the beginning. Their partners claim they have never had so much attention or love, that is, until the Poet sees some other horizon and sets sail for a new island on a distant shore.

The greatest difficulty for the Architect, the Achiever and the Sage is the ability to feel. The Poet in a sense gives life and animation to these three elements. However, for the one-dimensional Poet, feeling is not the problem. They feel everything. Many times, they are simply overwhelmed by their emotions. Because they lack the other elements, everything just floods in. They take mildly sarcastic remarks deeply to heart. Watching a news bulletin of a current tragedy can not only reduce them to tears, but also throw them right off balance. They don't handle any kind of suffering well, including their own.

Imagine our one-dimensional Poet as a passenger in the back of a truck speeding over a very bumpy road. The bumpy road is their life during challenging times. They feel battered and bruised by the sharp movements of the truck. Because they cannot see outside, they have no idea where the truck is going or why the truck is on the road in the first place. All they know is that they want the truck to stop in a quiet meadow so that they can get out and sit and watch the flowers.

The Architect and Sage would allow the Poet to look outside the truck and see why they are being bumped around. They may suggest it's time to travel on a different road. Their Achiever would provide the tenacity they need to overcome the bumps on the road. However, when challenges arise in the life of the one-dimensional Poet, they just want them to stop or go away. They long for an idyllic world where everyone is happy all the time.

The problem with wanting challenges to go away is that the very reason you experience challenges is to teach you something. The more you resist learning lessons in life, the more aggressively those lessons pursue you. In running away, you actually run in a circle, only to find your problem has compounded or changed form.

The Extraordinary Poet

One of my favorite poems that best describes the most sublime state of the Poet is by Christopher Morley. I remember reading this out one time to a very successful group of entrepreneurs, several of whom had slowly become 'hard-boiled'. There were quite a few tears as many realized what they had lost. Here is a portion of the poem:

TO A CHILD

The greatest poem ever known
Is one all poets have outgrown:
The poetry, innate, untold,
Of being only four years old.

Still young enough to be a part
Of Nature's great impulsive heart,
Born comrade of bird, beast, and tree
And unselfconscious as the bee—

And yet with lovely reason skilled
Each day new paradise to build;
Elate explorer of each sense,
Without dismay, without pretence!

In your unstained transparent eyes
There is no conscience, no surprise:
Life's queer conundrums you accept,
Your strange divinity still kept.

And Life, that sets all things in rhyme,
may make you poet, too, in time—
But there were days, O tender elf,
When you were Poetry itself!

The Sage

"Where is the wisdom we have lost in knowledge?"
—T. S. Eliot

Heightened Perception

I walked slowly into a warmly lit room in the company headquarters, taking in every detail. The space was long and rectangular. In the center of the room was a very expensive timber and glass coffee table. The whole place had the scent of prestige, money and power. If this room had a name, it would have been known as, 'The special meeting room to impress people'. If you worked for this company, this would be the room you would aspire to be in.

Around the coffee table were thick, luxurious lounge chairs, and on these were seated the top executives of the company.

I was there as a consultant. I hadn't been given any information on the company's financial position. All I had been told was that the company was looking to expand its horizons and develop its people. After I was formally introduced, the conversation moved to where the company saw itself heading and the bright prospects that the future could bring.

I knew from past experience that nothing really changes in life, business or relationships until you get to the truth. It seemed that this particular meeting was just going around in circles.

137

Finally, I leaned forward in my chair and said, 'Look, if it's okay with you, I'd like to cut straight to the chase.' I looked directly at the Chief Accountant. 'I bet if I looked at your books, I would find that if this company doesn't do something drastic in the next few years, you will be in liquidation.' An immense silence filled the room. The accountant looked at me in amazement and said, 'Yes, that's true. How did you know that?'

'I felt it,' I replied.

The accountant, puzzled, gently shook his head and said, 'Well how do you do that?'

I looked at him and replied, 'How do you not do that?'

What I meant was that this ability is a natural part of our makeup. We *naturally* have the ability to sense things but at some point many of us turn this sensibility off.

A few weeks later I was working with one of the head executives in her office when she asked me, 'Brendan, I notice that on many occasions you seem to have this uncanny ability to read situations and people like a book. You seem to know people's deepest thoughts. I feel that I lack that insight and it is limiting me in my life and career. How do you do it?'

'Okay,' I replied, shifting in my chair to directly face her. 'I want you to look at the desk and describe to me one object that is on the table.'

After she described a pen to me, I asked, 'So how do you know it's there?'

'I can see it,' she replied.

'So,' I continued. 'You trust what you see don't you? That's the first step in accessing your intuition or your knowing—you need to trust it as much as you trust all your other senses. If you heard a loud crash outside in the street you would have absolutely no doubt you heard it, so why doubt your intuition? When you awaken your Sage, it is like turning on another one of your senses. Just like you trust what you see, hear and smell, you learn to trust what you feel. Imagine walking around constantly doubting what you see. Imagine how confusing that would be. Well, it's also confusing when you doubt what you feel.'

She nodded in quiet, thoughtful agreement before I continued.

'You see, your intuition is like a friend. If you have a friend that constantly gives you advice that you never heed, what will your friend do?'

'They will either go away or keep quiet,' she answered.

'Exactly,' I replied. 'If you listen to your intuition and follow it, then that friend actually becomes stronger and more powerful. It becomes a very powerful ally. Intuition is a skill and like any skill it can be refined.'

The Sage's Blueprint

Sages revel in a detached, dispassionate outlook. Perched on their mountaintop they are able to view people without having to get involved in the emotional tides that engulf the rest of humanity. This is both their blessing and their curse, as they can be largely without emotion in relationships. Like the Sage's element of air, you sometimes feel you can't get hold of them, as it is often hard to know what they are thinking and feeling.

Sages derive a tremendous fulfillment from observing people and contemplating the deeper side of life. This detached state gives them tremendous insight and clarity of thinking. However, without the emotion of the Poet, it limits their relationships. The Sage prefers an environment that is uncomplicated and ordered. They are by nature aloof and often reserved. To them, the gregarious Poet is just a little too over the top. A Sage will often find the wild emotional swings of the Poet and the headlong rush of the Achiever a bit disturbing. Just like the advisor to a regent, the Sage sits in the background advising the Architect. They often are quite happy in their own company and their quiet reveries.

Avoiding Catastrophes and Disasters

The developed Sage understands the nature of the world—that we live in a dualistic world—a world with opposites. Summer/winter; hot/cold; day/night; light/dark; good people/ evil people; great times/bad times.

While the Sage recognizes that these forces exist, they want to place themselves where good things happen to them and avoid being dumped on by a big pile of crap. The one-dimensional Achiever looks for challenges to overcome. Their way is through. And you know, sometimes in life the only way is through—but not always! The Sage goes around or chooses not to be there when it's raining crap.

There are certain sports that force you to think this way. There has never been a book written called, 'The Seven Steps to Mastering Big Waves'. No big wave surfer would be arrogant enough to say they had mastered big waves, because they understand there are forces, like the ocean, that are infinitely bigger than them. No one in their right mind walks into the path of a tornado.

Some people in the self-help industry talk about being the master of your destiny. As if you can overcome the laws of the universe. I find a far more respectful approach is to navigate through the universe. Tell any sailor they should sail into a hurricane and just maintain a positive attitude. They would laugh at you.

One of the things you never do when you surf big waves is to paddle into the impact zone—the area where the waves break. This is putting yourself in harm's way. Yet people do this all the time in real life. Warren Buffett said, 'Be fearful when others are greedy and greedy when others are fearful.' Yet what happens in the real world? When the market is roaring to the top, everyone jumps in and when it is in free fall, everyone is jumping out. Sages are often contrarian—they rarely get swept away with the crowd and tend to be critical thinkers, evaluating a situation before they make their move.

How does the Sage support us in a very real and practical sense in the world? Sages understand that to stay stuck in one point of view is to risk stagnation. Stagnation can lead to great personal distress, as I witnessed first-hand when I was asked to lead a redevelopment program for government employees who were facing retrenchment.

I will never forget the first day of the course. As I walked to the front of the room and looked out at the faces of the workers, the message was the same from everyone. They were all frightened and bewildered. Many of them had been in their jobs for 20 or 30 years. None of them had ever expected this day would come. When they first became employees of the government they all assumed that it would be a job for life. In fact, for many of them, that was the very reason they joined in the first place. They wanted safety and security. They wanted to be in an environment that would never change.

Most of these people had bought an *absolute*. An absolute is when you hold a belief or position as certain and unchangeable. The following statements are good examples of absolutes:

"There is no reason for any individual to have a computer in the home."
—KEN OLSEN, *President of Digital Equipment Corporation in 1977*

"Louis Pasteur's theory of germs is ridiculous fiction."
—PIERRE PACHET, *Professor of Physiology at University of Toulouse in 1872*

When you *absolutely* know something to be correct, you no longer allow new possibilities and cease to be a lateral thinker.

The government workers were well-meaning people who had clung to an idea that was no longer relevant. Living in that absolute had not prepared them for the rapid change we are facing. That absolute had brought about the very thing they were trying to avoid—change.

Wanting the world to stay the same is folly. One thing is certain: the world is constantly changing. That is the only constant in the world—change. The weather is sunny one minute and cloudy the next. This endless change doesn't only apply to small things. Great continents and mountains are shifting position and shape. The whole universe is in a constant state of change.

These days, things are moving too fast for us to hold on to absolutes. In 1900 the eighth-largest company in America manufactured buggy whips. Where are they today? In this new millennium it will be imperative to embrace the Sage. Change is coming so quickly that we can no longer stick to old and outdated conditioning. For those who can embrace change and be fluid in their thinking it will be an amazing time.

The Sage gives you the ability to shift out of your preconditioned thinking and find new solutions. A lot of the time, what you perceive as the problem is not the actual problem. It is the way you *think* about the problem. Sometimes if you can expand your mind, the answer automatically comes to you.

I am sure you have had the experience of being stuck with a particular problem, with no possible solution in sight. You finally get so sick of it that you decide to do something else—go shopping, do the washing, anything to change the channel. As you're engaged in this new activity, out of the blue a solution that you would never have thought of comes to you. Ideas that have made millions have come from these kinds of moments.

In the world of the Sage there are no absolutes. Why? Because the Sage is more interested in wisdom than the accumulation of facts. When you strongly hold on to an absolute, your mind begins to contract. Try it. Begin thinking only in terms of absolutes for five minutes. Make some very strong mental assertions. People who are regarded as bigots are considered to be 'narrow-minded'. This is not just a figure of speech; the mind has the ability to contract and expand and begins to contract when someone only thinks in absolutes. Their mind actually narrows.

A true Sage realizes there are very few absolutes. Someone running may appear to be moving at a fast speed; however, compared to a cyclist they are slow. The cyclist compared to a car is slow, and what about a jet? So, what is fast?

Let's look at the concept of up and down. Where in the universe is there an up and down sign? Someone standing on the North Pole points toward their feet and says this is down. For someone on the South Pole the reverse is 'true'.

Fast, small, large, up and down are concepts. They only become real when compared with something else.

The Sage who can appreciate alternative viewpoints is open to lateral thinking and new possibilities.

Is That a Fact?

About 15 years ago I took all the beliefs I could think of—all of the beliefs that I was consciously aware of—and with each belief I asked one question: 'How do I know this to be true?' With the vast majority of my beliefs, I came to the conclusion that I did not know them to be true. They were not facts, they were opinions. Yes, opinions not facts. Here is what most people do. They have an opinion, and they turn it into a fact. A fixed construct. Or if they are a bit more discerning, they have a belief in something and then they gather evidence to support that belief. A person I know believes the ultra-rich are nasty—she has gathered an impressive array of evidence to support her conclusion. When I talk about how many of them are huge philanthropists—well she just can't get it. She knows how that part of the world works—at least she thinks she does. Now, with that belief, what are the odds of her becoming rich? It is very difficult to have what you judge. If you judge the successful, then it's hard to be one of them. I have a saying: 'every belief has a consequence'. Your beliefs can liberate you or be your doom. Have you noticed how many people have very fixed beliefs? There is not a lot of wiggle room for new opinions and seeing the world in a fresh way.

An Exercise in Lateral Thinking

One of the ways I used to train my children to have more lateral thinking ability was to give them certain exercises. Here is one of the puzzles I used to give them when they were little. Try it out.

An empty train pulls into a station and 20 people get on the train. It pulls into the next station and five people get off the train. At the next station, 10 people get on the train. The next station, 15 people get on the train. The next station, five people get off the train and at the last station, 10 people get on the train.

The question is, how many times did the train stop? The answer of course is six. However, the answer is largely irrelevant. What is more important is how people follow the problem. When I give most people the problem, they start counting the numbers of people who get on the train. The reason they do this is that everything in their educational training has led them to follow this kind of procedure. A lot of our education is the accumulation of facts that we repeat back at exam time in the hope of getting good grades. Not a lot of our education is about thinking outside the square.

Thomas Edison was sent home with a note saying, 'This boy is too stupid to learn'. Yet Edison became a multimillionaire. The sculptor Rodin was the worst student in the school and regarded by his uncle as being incapable of being educated. All of these people were well-endowed with the Sage. It was this element that allowed them to think outside the square and be an inspiration to the world.

Being in the Right Place at the Right Time

When you are in the right place at the right time, you are in touch with your own inner Sage. Whether they are a legendary investor who seems to have a 'feel' for the market, or an entrepreneur who recognizes an opportunity, or a sailor who senses the changing weather, the Sage is in tune with their environment.

I remember listening to a talk by the great mountaineer Doug Scott, who has climbed all the 8,000-meter peaks in the world. As he explained his adventures through his presentation, he pointed out all the mountaineers who had died over the years. By my count, it seemed nearly half of the people in those photographs had perished in the mountains. Finally, someone voiced the question of how he had survived into his fifties when so many others had not. In his quiet, unassuming manner he leaned towards the crowd and said, 'Because I listen. If it doesn't feel right, I do something else.'

He explained that the final decision-maker is his intuition. If he gets a feeling to abort an attempt to the summit, then no matter how good the conditions look he will turn back. On the other hand, when climbing Everest, he got the feeling to make the final ascent at three in the morning. As it turned out, the weather held just long enough to reach the summit and return to the camp.

You don't have to be a mountaineer to use appropriate timing. *Appropriate timing takes the struggle out of life.* Sages have the ability to determine when to make their move. Like a great football quarterback, they stand holding the ball looking for the perfect opportunity to throw. Around them chaos reigns, with people running in all directions, but the quarterback stands quietly centered, waiting for the right time to act.

With their ability to perceive appropriate timing, the Sage makes life easy and graceful. It is this lesson of ease and grace that the Achiever needs to learn if they want to achieve holistic success.

A person I know who works in sales is a classic Achiever. He goes for everything like a bull at a gate, and often uses up twice as much energy than if he were to wait for the appropriate time. He rubs many people up the wrong way because he is not able to subjugate his ego and he barges in where Sages fear to tread. He means well but he starts becoming pushy and pretty soon, customers start looking for the exit. Being a classic Achiever, all he sees is *outcome* and the sign above the customer's head that spells 'target'. He often wonders why people get upset with him and start becoming edgy. 'Oh no, here comes that guy again.' If he were to turn his Sage on, he would be able to determine what his customers really want.

When the Achiever combines with the Sage, it produces action and timing. It makes your passage in the world much easier.

The Power of the Invisible

Air is the element you cannot see. All the other elements previously mentioned—fire, earth and water—can be seen. Air, like intuition and wisdom, is invisible to the senses. However, just because it is invisible does not mean it isn't there. In our culture we put great emphasis on what can be seen, touched and felt, and tend to distrust things that are not so tangible. 'I need proof before I am going to trust something like intuition,' is often the unspoken catch-cry.

Air has the greatest mobility of all the elements. Like true wisdom and intuition, it is free to move in any direction. Air will enter unseen into the smallest crack and sit in the shadows, like the watchful Sage. The Sage is quite content to let the Achiever and the Architect take center stage. It prefers to remain invisible, watching and waiting in the background. You can often spot the Sage at a meeting or a party. They are the ones who appear dispassionate and reserved, but nothing escapes their attention. They wait until everyone has spoken before entering the fray with a stunning observation or comment showing perceptive lateral thinking.

Sages are masters of timing. They often take people with an undeveloped Sage by surprise because they have a tremendous capacity to wait before making their move. Sports or businesspeople who abound in this element use it to pull a strategy out of the bag that is completely unexpected, thus giving them the winning edge.

A good example of this, and a real learning experience for me, was one of the first times I went rock climbing. We were halfway up a 300-meter cliff face and on a vertical pitch of about 35 meters. I could feel the sun on my back and the heat reflecting off the rocks, on to my hands and legs. My arms were beginning to tremble with the effort and sweat was dripping into my eyes. I was talking to myself, 'Come on, push, you can do it, let's go.' It was really taking all my focus and effort.

Even though I was securely roped and in little danger, I was clinging to the cracks in the rocks as if my life depended on it. As I finally clambered over the edge puffing and panting and congratulating myself for having made it, my friend said, 'Check this out.' As I got to my knees and looked up, there were two women climbers on the next pitch above. They were moving at a very easy but rapid, fluid pace. What was so stunning about them was that they weren't even breaking a sweat. They were just effortlessly snaking over the rocks, no straining, no grunting and heaving, just finding the perfect handhold at the perfect time. They were in the flow—ease and grace. A small smile crept over my face and I shook my head in silent admiration.

Developing Intuitive Power

THE GREAT QUALITY OF THE SAGE IS INTUITION

Have you ever gone into a shop and tried on that shirt with the stripes and spots? As you're standing in front of the mirror with your face all screwed up wondering how quickly you can take off this ghastly covering, over walks the sales assistant.

'Oh, that looks wonderful on you.'

You try to smile, but really, you're cringing. It is obvious their Sage is either temporarily asleep or has gone on a long vacation. If their Sage was alert, they would have noticed everything about you and what you felt.

With a strong Sage, the sales assistant would just know what you were feeling. They would be more interested in steering you towards something you liked. They would also sense, after just a brief conversation, what budget you had. Rather than causing any embarrassment they would suggest certain options.

Intuition is the first great quality of the Sage. Your intuition is the voice of guidance. It has been referred to as a 'gut feeling' or a 'hunch'. Your intuition warns you of impending danger or allows you to identify a situation that feels just right. It is a powerful ally and to be without it is a serious handicap in life. It is a valuable guide and a dear friend. It is the primary quality and tool of the Sage. The Sage wielding the scepter of intuition speaks in the ear of the Architect and the Achiever. It cautions them of impending roadblocks and alerts them to amazing opportunities; legendary investors and entrepreneurs who have harnessed its capabilities have made billions of dollars.

There are two voices within you that express themselves. The first is your inner dialogue and the second is your intuition.

Your inner dialogue is the running commentary that manifests as inner chatter. Your intuition is a different voice altogether. For some people their intuition is a spoken voice. For most people though, it is a deep sense of feeling or knowing.

A good example of the two voices would be to imagine you had just finished a splendid three-course meal. As you sit there replete and completely satisfied, you notice there is one large slice of your favorite chocolate cake left on the table. Your internal dialogue might start saying, 'Yes, yes, yes,' while your intuition is saying, 'If you eat that cake, you're going to be ill.'

I am often asked how I work out the difference between my inner dialogue and my intuition. Practices like meditation still the mind and the inner dialogue. As your mind becomes clearer and more focused by following these practices, you automatically know when your intuition is speaking. However, sometimes the messages may not be so clear. If that happens, I proceed toward the situation but keep listening to the messages.

Recently, I was approached by a friend of mine to be part of a very large business venture. When I looked at the venture it seemed a fantastic opportunity, but as I began to proceed, all avenues to getting the project off the ground were blocked.

Opportunities that at first seemed promising finished in a dead-end. It felt as if there was no synchronicity at all. After several of these experiences I asked myself if these were merely hurdles we had to leap over, or if they were a genuine indication that this was not what I was meant to be doing. The more I *felt* into the situation, the more I became convinced that this venture was not for me. I felt that it was pulling me off my real track and my purpose.

I spent about two weeks of part-time work on the project before I finally arrived at this conclusion. I decided at that point to walk away, in spite of the fact that part of my inner dialogue was saying that I was walking away from a large sum of money. FOMO, 'fear of missing out', has nailed many an entrepreneur. Months later the venture finally ground to a halt. If I hadn't walked away when I did, I would have wasted months of time.

If you aren't sure whether it is your intuition or your inner dialogue that is speaking, you can listen to the quality of your inner voice. If it is an endless chatter in your mind, then maybe you are hearing your inner dialogue rather than your intuition. Your intuition usually arises from a place of stillness within you.

Spotting Money-Making Opportunities

'Reality is merely an illusion, albeit a very persistent one.'

—ALBERT EINSTEIN

Seeing the world in a different way, and the ability to see money-making opportunities that others do not, is not some namby-pamby concept. It is based on biological and scientific fact...

There is a part of the brain called the Reticular Activating System (RAS), which among other things acts as a data filtration system. The numbers vary from reference to reference, but according to popular wisdom, we are being bombarded with millions of 'bits' of information every second through the five senses. If we were consciously aware of all those bits of information, we would go insane. Can you imagine being aware of every sound that's happening around you, every object in your line of vision, every sensation on your skin or everything that you brush past and every movement you make? You'd never get any sleep for a start!

So as human beings we delete the vast majority of the information. Of the millions of bits of possible information that we could process, it's estimated that we actually process less than 1%! We are deleting or not even processing over 99% of all the possible data out there.

What we delete is also based on our beliefs, attitudes, values, past experiences, social expectations and conditioning. These things influence what we believe is 'normal', and probably more importantly, what we believe is possible. The RAS is the filter system that decides what we become aware of and what happily floats past.

You'll have experienced this before. Let's say you decide to buy a car and you've chosen a red convertible sports car. You're driving your old car through the city and all of a sudden you see them everywhere. What's going on? Has a large shipment of red convertibles just descended into the city or were they given away on a breakfast radio show or something? No, as soon as you decided that you liked that car, your RAS filter system included that in your awareness. The cars were always there— you just didn't see them because they were not important to you. If you ask a woman who is pregnant if she has noticed that there seems to be a lot of pregnant women around, she will always agree that there appears to be an increase in pregnant women. However, it is because pregnant women are now on her radar. As an entrepreneur with a high-powered business she noticed different things, but now that she's expecting a child her radar has changed to include her business and her new baby, therefore her experience of the world around her has changed with it.

If you are a centerline Achiever, with very little Sage, you will perceive the world as a place where success is achieved through a lot of hard slog. Your worldview believes that 'magical thinking' and opportunities to get to the top easily are flakey. You will be bewildered by people that seem to be in the right place at the right time. 'Maybe they are just lucky,' you say. The Sage expects to spot opportunities on a regular basis. Their brain is hardwired to look for opportunities, while the Achiever does it the hard way.

Your brain, through the RAS, searches for information or things that are relevant to you obtaining your objective. If you are wired to see the world as a place of struggle, where the only way to the top is working 100 hours a week, then that will be your filter. When you make it to the top, you will conclude that struggle against the odds is the only way. Yes, you do have to work, however, the Sage likes to get there in the easiest way possible. There is a saying that states that the opportunity of a lifetime comes around every two weeks. And I totally believe that's true. It's just that most people don't see those opportunities because their RAS is not set up to look for them!

The new science of quantum physics is also illustrating that we have far more control over what happens in our lives than previously assumed. Quantum physics is basically the science of the very small. While classic Newtonian physics explains the universe very well when it comes to falling apples and spinning planets, when scientists turned their attention to the very small, they found that these accepted explanations didn't work at the sub-atomic level.

Without getting overly technical, studies in quantum physics have shown that what we experience is very much influenced by what we think and feel. Studies all around the world are proving time and again that by turning our attention and focus in a particular direction we somehow influence the results toward that expectation.

Professor William Tiller of Stanford University has conducted experiments with seasoned meditators to see if their intention could alter reality. In one experiment he got a very simple electronic box and asked the meditators to concentrate their intention on the box. The intention was to raise the pH of water. These boxes, along with control boxes (with no meditation directed toward them), were then placed next to water taken from the same source. There was no change to the water in the control boxes, yet the water subjected to meditation changed in pH value. Changing pH is not an easy task and the chances of this occurring naturally were millions to one.

The idea that we have much more power over what happens in our life simply by directing our intentions is not new. What is new is that science in now beginning to prove what many people have suspected.

If this new science is proving the unquestionable influence that our thoughts have on outcome, then what is the answer in relation to using our Sage to get to the top? The centerline Achiever wants to take credit for getting to the top. The Achiever gets prepared, fills their backpack with food and water, then hikes up a difficult mountain. Directly above them the Sage is on the chairlift looking down thinking, 'What the hell are they doing that for?' When the Achiever gets to the top they congratulate themselves for the hard work and feel a great sense of achievement. The Sage wants to take the easiest path possible to get to the top.

Want to be more like the Sage? First you have to define what success actually means to you. Is it money? Is it recognition from others or yourself? If it is recognition then you may have a tendency to choose a difficult path so when you finally make it, you can prove to yourself and others you are okay. We talked about this in the Architect section. It is crucial to know exactly where you are going so you can put your intention behind it.

Part of achieving success is defining what success looks like to you. There's a great conversation between Alice and the Cheshire Cat in *Alice in Wonderland*. Alice wants directions and asks the cat, 'Would you tell me, please, which way I ought to go from here?' To which the cat replies, 'That depends a good deal on where you want to get to.' Alice says, 'I don't much care where.' The cat responds, 'Then it doesn't matter which way you go.'

Let's take an example. You want money. You want to do it with more Sage. Repeat after me: 'I want to make the most money, in the shortest amount of time, with the least amount of effort.' Yes, you absolutely will have to use your Achiever to get to that goal as well. There is work involved, but the Sage is less interested in 'you' doing it. It wants to get on the chairlift, not hike up the mountain.

If you don't know where you're going or what you're trying to achieve, then how will you know when you've arrived? You are always going somewhere; your current thoughts, actions and behaviors are plotting a course all the time. But unless you take conscious control of that process, you may end up deeply disappointed with the destination and how you got there.

Expand Your Thinking So You Can Spot Amazing Opportunities for Greater Financial Success

A champion ice skater told me a very interesting story. She said that when she skated on a crowded ice rink, she never saw the people on the ice rink, she saw the gaps in between the people.

It made me think. The few times I have skated I was hopeless at it. I always saw all the obstacles whereas she saw all the opportunities. In the business arena you need to see the gaps that other people do not see. For example, most business owners (or people in general) are just busy trying to get through their 'to-do list'. Their focus is like the amateur skater who is concentrating on the people rather than the gaps. Start by asking the question, 'What do I want to achieve?' My ice skating friend wanted to find a clear course to where she wanted to go.

Expand your thinking around that idea so that you can identify the gaps. Fortunes have been made by people that could see the gaps! Cheung Yan became a billionaire by seeing something that was right in front of everyone's nose but invisible to everyone else. So how did she do it? She was made redundant and with her redundancy payout she decided to plug a gap in the market. She had been trading paper as part of her previous job and put two and two together.

All of the white goods products being produced have one thing in common—they all need a cardboard box. Rather than use trees to make her cardboard, she came up with a novel idea. Cheung Yan looked to America. In America they had a problem—too much waste paper. So, Cheung Yan bought the waste at a knock-down price, she then shipped that paper back to recycling plants in China and made cardboard boxes out of it to supply the Chinese market. Those goods were then shipped back to America and sold, and so the cycle began again.

At every stage of the process she made money. She spotted two gaps: a problem in the US and an opposite problem in China, and made money solving both. And she is helping the environment in the process, as the same resource is recycled indefinitely. It's brilliant—in fact, it's so brilliant you wonder why no one thought of it before. **Don't think like everyone else!** How do you put yourself in this state of mind? It is very difficult if someone is a centerline Achiever and constantly on the work treadmill. Some of my greatest ideas have come when I am doing nothing or in inspirational places like the ocean, the mountains or beautiful parts of Europe. Take the time to vacation in amazing places, spend time in nature and do what renews and inspires you. That is often when the ideas come to me.

The Sage's Toolkit

Seeing Things As They Are

If you want to have a high level of mastery of your intuition, you must be willing to see a situation as it really is, rather than what you would like it to be. The openhearted Poet trusts everyone. *Highly intuitive Sages don't trust people; rather, they trust what they feel about people.* In this way, they avoid delusion. Great entrepreneurs have this ability. It seems simple but it is not! It takes courage to see things and people as they truly are, because there is a certain false sense of happiness or safety created when someone looks through their delusion filter.

Delusion occurs when you don't see a situation or person as they really are, and works in two different ways. One way operates through naivety, for example when someone who is naive trusts the wrong person. The other way can be seen in someone who has, for example, had a very bad relationship experience and believes that no one is to be trusted. They come to a conclusion based on their past experiences. People with a highly developed Sage look past their filter and see someone as they really are.

A study was done by neuroscientists, David Hubel and Torsten Wiesel, in which the experimenters raised two groups of kittens. The first group was raised in an environment solely containing vertical stripes. The second group was raised in an environment where everything contained horizontal stripes. When the kittens became cats, they were placed in a normal environment.

The cats that had been raised in a vertically striped world were unable to see anything that was horizontal. If, for example, there was a low-lying coffee table, they would bump into the tabletop. They were fine to navigate chair legs but unable to see the seat of the chair. The group that were raised in a horizontal world, on the other hand, were unable to see anything vertical and would bump into the table legs. They could easily see the seat of the chair and would jump on to it if they wanted to nap. The cats had been conditioned to perceive the world in a certain way. All of us have been conditioned to see the world from our own distinct viewpoints. The art of having a high level of intuition and ability to spot amazing opportunities is to go beyond your conditioning. It entails perceiving a person or situation without being influenced by your conditioned mind. It means using your intuition to directly see a particular scenario.

With a high level of intuition, you are able to do this with everyone in your world. Even the people close to you. If you hold one thing in delusion or fantasy, it affects your entire sense of reality. It is like wanting to be extremely fit and running 10 miles every morning, then smoking a packet of cigarettes every night. Those cigarettes are going to affect your fitness. Even if you increase your fitness program, unless you ditch the cigarettes you will never really achieve peak fitness. It's the same with your intuition. If you hold one thing in delusion, it will cloud your intuition in other areas.

To get out of delusional thinking, you need to see people and situations as they really are, rather than what you would like them to be. As I said, it takes a lot of courage to do this. Human beings often hold delusional thinking as a way of protecting themselves. I remember talking to someone who refused to believe that their partner would let them down. Even though deep down they intuitively knew the truth, it was too painful for them to face. Later, when the relationship broke up, they had to face the truth, which was that their partner had never been committed to the relationship.

Delusional thinking can also inhibit you from having a strong sense of self. A person I know, who is a classic Poet, often felt taken for granted in her relationships with people. She felt that people treated her as a doormat because she allowed them to walk all over her. She trusted people that any discerning person would never trust. She is now learning how to establish healthy boundaries and stand up for herself, which is giving her a sense of strength and confidence. Essentially, she is awakening her Sage and her Achiever. When the Sage and the Achiever form an alliance it gives you a very powerful form of protection. The Sage evaluates people's true intentions and the Achiever backs up those evaluations by creating firm boundaries.

A friend of mine who is very successful in business has the ability to see everything as it really is. If he is looking at a new proposal, he never allows himself to be swayed by hype or popular opinion. It is one of the traits that has made him successful.

Of course, you also need your Architect to see the person's potential, however, the Sage is interested in seeing things as they really are. When you develop this ability to a high degree, it allows you to attract people who can aid your plans and help fulfill your goals.

One Big Key to Creativity

I want to discuss something that is rarely, if ever, talked about. It is, I believe, the key to deep productivity and more importantly, creativity. It is not for the faint of heart. I have recommended it to others, but most have never done it.

The secret is ... (wait for it) ... boredom. Yep, bear with me. In today's world most people have been reduced from human beings into human doings.

All of nature is cyclic, and yet humans have departed from this. People have often wondered how I get through so much work in so little time. When I am on, I am completely on. However, I have also spent considerable amounts of time when I completely switch off.

Most people think of downtime as doing things like watching a movie, checking their phone, reading a book or playing a video game, but that isn't really switching off. I have had times when for weeks on end I will not check emails or phone messages—where I only hang out in nature.

After a period of months of full-on work, I can tell you that the first few days are difficult—I get bored. This is where most people check out. They get distracted—they have to start doing something. The boredom feels painful and they just want it to go away. The key is going through this to arrive at what I call the 'let go state'.

The great author, F. Scott Fitzgerald, once said, 'Boredom is not an end product, but rather an early stage in life and art. You have to go by, or past, or through boredom, as through a filter, before the clear product emerges.'

Mary Mann, a researcher into boredom, found that scientifically there are great benefits in going through boredom, and that it is something that we should embrace.

I like to do this especially when I have completed a business cycle that I might have been on for years. After finally leaving one business, I decided to 'go feral'. My wife and I spent months camped out in two million acres of national forest, next to a beautiful winding river in Colorado. At night the only sounds were the crackling fire, the river and the howling cries of wild coyotes. The first couple of weeks I found really difficult. The boredom was intense. However, gradually we adjusted to the rhythm of nature and my mind crawled to a stop. It was a time of great happiness. When we finally emerged back in the business world, the business accelerated like a rocket, because we were so clear and renewed about our direction. I think a lot of people are dragging themselves through life on half a tank of fuel. Going into nature and switching off can be a time of great renewal. We get to see what is important and what is a distraction.

There are four great benefits I have found when I have been willing to switch off from the world and truly immerse myself in nature:

1. It has created a tremendous clarity about the direction I need to take in my life. I believe all great endeavors start with 'listening' to where we are meant to go, rather than forcing ourselves down a dead-end road.
2. The power of my seminars, work and creativity has always radically jumped after such a period.
3. My happiness has jumped significantly. I believe one of the reasons that people in the Western world are unhappy is that they will not go through the 'let go cycle'.
4. Some of my biggest ideas have emerged during these times. Some of these ideas have made me serious money; so much for the theory that I was wasting my time—it was time well spent.

As I said, this approach is not for the faint of heart. I would get a better result if I just tried to sell you the latest social media strategy to make a million in five minutes—but that wouldn't be the truth. I believe getting really, really clear before you start launching any strategy is infinitely more powerful than some get-rich-quick scheme. So many people are unaware of just how overwhelmed they are with unnecessary burdens and beliefs. Many carry invisible loads that are weighing them down and making the journey to the top slow and painful. Which leads us to a very important subject...

The Principal of Non-Engagement

Occasionally, perhaps a few times a year, I'll tune into talkback radio and listen to all the things that people are upset about.

I hear people ranting and raving about all sorts of things. They talk about such drivel as 'the irresponsible youth' (by the way, the older generation have been saying for centuries how youth is going to the dogs) or politics AND yet they don't DO anything about it. They just engage their mind in it. It's a guaranteed way to destroy not only your time but also your levels of peace and clarity of mind. And you do need clarity of mind to make money. If your head is full of stuff, it's hard to think straight.

The usual conversations are about the latest news item that is running hot. These people have obviously not mastered the principal of non-engagement. Now, before you get on your high horse, I am not saying don't engage in important issues. Of course, we all have to take responsibility and do everything we can about the problems. But that's my point—do everything you can and then stop thinking about it.

So many of us get upset and wound up about issues, but all we ever do about it is bitch. We might not be sad enough to get on talkback radio, but we bitch to our friends or our family and bore the pants off the neighbors with our constant whining about whatever the hot topic of the day is.

What's the point? It's a complete waste of your time. So my answer is, do something about it or don't think about it. If you're upset about not making any money in your business, do something about it or stop thinking about it. If you're upset about the government, do something about it or stop thinking about it. Ideally, do something about it and then stop thinking about it. But whining won't change anything! You only have a certain amount of attention units in your brain and if you load them up with garbage that you have no control over, then there's nothing left to focus on the things you have got control over.

If you've got a problem, do something. If you're upset about the economy, do something about it. If you can't do anything about it, forget about it. If you've got a problem with the starving kids in an undeveloped country, do something about it. Go and help or donate money, which is something I am a big believer in. If you are unwilling to do anything, what is the point in thinking about it? Sure, you may not be able to single-handedly change poverty in Africa but as Margaret Mead once said, 'Never doubt that a small group of thoughtful, committed citizens can change the world. Indeed, it is the only thing that ever has.' Sponsor a child or sponsor a school or do something that really makes a difference.

Or you could focus on making a ton of money so you can really make a financial contribution that would help change things.

This isn't about being heartless, it's about head space. If something is bothering you, fix it and move on. Don't let your focus and attention be robbed by something that you can't change. For example, I went into a service station recently to fill up and I used a certain credit card to pay. As soon as I put it down, I could see the guy behind the counter almost recoil! He started making some comments about it and he was obviously very resentful. The card indicated a certain degree of wealth and that upset him. I could feel myself getting annoyed. But I have two options here: engage or delete. And I hit delete. In the end I chose to feel empathy for him. He was angry at me because he hated his job and I represented what he didn't think he could have. I get that, but I'm not going to waste my time stewing about it and getting upset.

The same with spending huge chunks of your day immersed in the news. If you believe you can pour into you all that negativity on the news and remain unaffected, then check this out. Scientists did a study where they got people to walk down a long hall and unscramble five sentences that were jumbled. In each sentence there were two words—'old age'. Then they measured how long it took for them to walk back up the hall. When asked to repeat the exercise of unraveling the sentences, this time without the words 'old age', all the subjects walked back up the hall quicker than the previous time. The conclusion was that even though the subjects were not consciously aware of any change, sub-consciously they were affected. What you put in your head has an effect! As a guy that is regarded as an expert on marketing, let me tell you a little secret. The reason that they print bad news is because that is what sells. They have tried selling 'good news' and it does not sell. So basically, they scour the world for bad news and print that.

Here is what I do. I subscribe to some very good newsletters where I get all the raw data, without the negative slant, and some good newsletters that provide an educated, economic picture. This, by the way, actually saves me a lot of time as well as giving me a much more accurate picture of what is going on. Be careful what you engage with. Engage with the wrong things and they will rob you of your time and energy.

A Quantum Leap—How I Doubled My Income...

Want to know how I doubled my income even though I had a crippling injury?

Here is a great tool in the Sage's kit. One of the most powerful things you can do to have a quantum leap is ask what I call 'directed questions'. Directed questions are questions directed to your subconscious mind. They are not questions you can figure out with your rational mind. Asking, 'What is one plus one?' is something your rational mind can easily figure out and obviously not a directed question.

There are certain directed questions that are incredibly powerful and can literally open new doorways for your entire life. Personally, I love this technique and have found it incredibly helpful in my life.

If you remember, in the Achiever section I talked about how I was almost crippled with a debilitating injury, where I was on crutches for months. What I didn't mention was that my income doubled during this time, which should have been impossible. Prior to the injury I was doing a lot of live events and traveling the world. After the injury, the ability to operate this way was extremely difficult. So, I asked a directed question: 'How can I double my income without being on the road?'

Now, this part is crucial. I didn't ask this question once and forget about it. I asked it for days with a fierce intention to know the answer. I was committed to knowing the answer. I did NOT try and figure it out. I just asked the question repeatedly and let my subconscious mind go to work. Days later the answer popped into my mind. It was something totally outside the box and allowed me to work from home doing a special kind of online program.

There are some particular directed questions I call The Five Power Questions:

1. How can I add more value to my customers or clients?
2. How can I double my income?
3. How can I work less and earn more?
4. How can I double my leads?
5. How can I double my sales?

When you are stuck with a problem you can't solve, this can be incredibly powerful. This technique has led to a lot of breakthroughs.

Traits that Self-Sabotage

THE ONE-DIMENSIONAL SAGE

Have you ever looked from above at a trail of ants? As you watch the ants, it is like peering into another world. This is often how the Sage sees the world of human relationships.

People whose only aspect is the Sage are very aloof. They tend to stand back and observe the world from a distant perspective. They see all the comings and goings of humanity, but they never feel emotionally involved. To them it is a vast movie, fascinating, interesting and intriguing. If the Sage lacks the Poet, then the problem is further exacerbated. They simply find it difficult to feel, and become detached from those around them. This, of course, plays havoc with their relationships. In the beginning, they are admired for their incredible insight into problems. Grateful partners delight at their ability to get right to the heart of the matter. However, as time goes on, their calm dispassion becomes a thorn under the skin.

One of the keys in relationships that you will need to succeed, or create truly amazing customer service, is the sharing of yourself. The one-dimensional Sage finds this a daunting task. Because of their tremendous insight, they see everyone's foibles. However, without the Poet's compassion, they fail to realize that we are all a work in progress.

The one-dimensional Sage, who does not have the benefit of the Achiever, never really rises to their potential. They often have a great depth to them, and they know exactly what they should do, but the problem is actually doing it. Without the drive of the

Achiever, there is no incentive to go out and make something happen. They might see an opportunity right in front of them, but without the Achiever they find it hard to dive through that window.

The Extraordinary Sage

COMMUNING WITH CLOUDS

This almost got edited out of the book because it is outside a lot of people's reality. I think a lot of people would find it unbelievable, a work of fiction, yet it did happen; it is a true story. It does not directly relate to being an entrepreneur, but in a way it does...

We were just outside of Taos, New Mexico, on a very cold mid-winter's day. It was alternating between rain, sleet and the occasional flurry of snow. Our group was driven inside the house by the freezing conditions. We had all come to participate in a Native American sweat lodge, which was to be run by a medicine man I will call Martin, who lived on a reservation several hours away. (A sweat lodge is a ceremony, which physically feels a bit like a sauna, but has a very powerful atmosphere.)

Martin looks like many other Native Americans. His long black hair falls down his back. If you saw him in a crowd, you probably wouldn't even notice him—medium height, round face with inquisitive, owl-like eyes. He tends to be a listener rather than a talker and has a very quiet, unassuming manner.

It was about an hour before we had to light the fire to heat up the large rocks that were to be brought into the confines of the lodge itself. As I looked around the group, I could see some of the members were wondering how we could light a fire in these cold, wet, sleeting and snowing conditions.

When Martin came into the house that day, many people didn't even see him. He wandered over to a small cluster of people standing just outside the kitchen.

I was in this small group, along with a person who had joined the tour by the name of Brian. We used to joke with Brian that he was so conservative, banks would reject his employment application because he was too straight. Brian had come on the trip to broaden his horizons. He was a bit skeptical about all this stuff, but he was genuinely giving it his best shot.

Brian struck up a conversation with Martin and they were talking amicably enough when Martin looked at Brian and the rest of the group and said, 'You'll have to excuse me, I need to go and handle the weather.'

Brian's expression was one of disbelief, as if someone had said, 'We are eating roasted bats for dinner.' Now at this point, the sleet and snow were belting down in every direction as far as the eye could see.

Martin went outside and began to chant quietly to himself and the elements.

About 25 minutes later a ragged hole appeared in the clouds directly above us. For several miles in every direction, it ceased to rain or snow. Everywhere outside that rough circle, the weather continued to come down. It stayed that way while we lit the fire and throughout the several hours of the ceremony. About half an hour after we finished, we were covered in flurries of snow. It had all happened so inconspicuously that some of the group hadn't even noticed.

What was the reason for this 'miracle?' Because this group had come such a long way and with genuine good intention in their hearts, Martin just 'wanted to help the people'. Brian still talks about it to this day.

Martin is someone with the element of the Sage at a very rarefied level. He knows that he is part and parcel of the great dance of life. Rather than seeing himself as separate to all of nature, he actually experiences nature as part of himself. He experientially knows he is part of the great web of life. This is not a theory; it is a way of being. The elements of nature are like friends to him.

The consummate Sage is in the flow of all things. They do not barge through brick walls, they move in harmony with everything around them with elegance and grace. They want to get to the goal with the least resistance and drama.

Some people find the story of Martin and the weather absolutely amazing. While I am amazed, I have seen things like this many times, in several countries. Why? Because I expect to see them.

The key to having more experiences like this is to be open to them. Quite a few people close themselves off from other experiences because it is too confronting. They want to feel safe in a world that is structured and ordered. It is a way of staying in control. However, the world isn't fixed. It is constantly changing. When you let go of control, you realize there is nothing to fear.

It is like sitting in a large room, facing a corner. As you stare at the walls, you believe that all that exists in your universe is this one corner.

Along comes the Sage, who takes you by the hand and says, 'Yes, that is a very interesting corner, but if you just change your angle of vision you will see an entire room.' You turn your head and all of a sudden you see an array of wonders you had never noticed before.

How is all of this relevant in the real world? Imagine the kind of opportunities you could spot as an entrepreneur. Imagine the lateral thinking you would have in the marketing of those opportunities. Imagine being more in the flow and having less struggle.

In the Wealth Secrets Club Membership, I show you a lot of lateral 'sage-like' strategies to make your life easier, that can lead to escaping the endless grind. The membership site/app, includes 100+ video and audio tutorials and how-to manuals. Plus, so much more…

You can find out more at **WealthSecretsClub.com**

Spirit

I have occasionally had people say something like this:
'I really like your message, but I often wonder why you talk about all this stuff.'

If you need a pragmatic answer, then I will leave you with the following to ponder. Marianne Williamson said: *'You can use the force that makes planets move and flowers grow, or you can do it all yourself.'*

The Powerful Presence

We had been awake all night. It was the birth of my first daughter, and the small group who were assembled in the birthing room was working together as a cohesive unit, quietly and efficiently taking care of all the necessary details.

Leading up to this birth, none of us realized that on this particular day we were to experience a lesson that would alter our perception of the way we viewed people and the world around us.

As the rest of the city lay asleep, we were immersed in another world. The intensity of the moment had banished all thoughts of the past and the future. We were all firmly rooted in the present. It seemed nothing else existed outside

175

that small, dimly lit room. (If you are wondering what has this got to do with being a successful entrepreneur, read on).

Conversations were brief and muted. All of us were witnessing one of life's greatest miracles—birth. The contractions became more frequent and powerful. I looked around the room and could see that everyone's concentration had risen to another level, adding to the mounting pressure. The intensity was so thick you could have cut it with a knife.

Finally, the moment arrived. The baby slid out uttering a little moaning cry, 'Oh, oh, oh.' It sounded for the entire world like, 'I'm here, thank God that's over, I'm here.' There was no distress in the sound. Rather, it was as if the baby was relieved it was all over. After the baby was helped up on to her mother's stomach, we waited for a while to let her settle.

Twenty minutes later I took her in my hands. I could feel the incredibly soft, silky skin and the almost weightless feel of her body. Very slowly I eased her into a tub of water that was slightly warmer than the amniotic fluid in the womb. Seven adults were on one side of the big bath while I was on the other. It was then that something completely unexpected occurred.

As she lay in the water, she opened her eyes completely. Being 20 minutes old, she couldn't move her head, but her eyes moved to each person in the group. She looked at each person for up to several minutes at a time. This was not the fuzzy-eyed, defocused look of a newborn, but the intense and intent gaze of a completely aware being. After looking deeply into the eyes of one person she would move to the next person and gaze profoundly into their eyes. Throughout this time her eyes never wandered vacantly into space. They remained firmly focused on each individual. Looking into the baby's eyes was like staring into the depths of a naked soul — a vast, powerful presence.

It was completely apparent to everyone that she was the oldest and wisest being in the room. It was as if we were in the presence of someone who was centuries old.

It took a couple of days for this to change. After two days, she became a baby, manifesting all the innocence of every newborn.

In India they say that at the moment of birth, you begin to forget who you really are and become lost in the illusion of the world. What you forget is that you are a spiritual being. You begin to slowly turn your attention to the external events in the world and identify with them. We see ourselves as our body, emotions, feelings and achievements. The more we identify with all these things, the more our true essence becomes clouded and obscured. We travel through life feeling that something is missing; that no matter how much we achieve, something eludes us. Many people never realize that what eludes them is closer than their own breath, nearer than their own skin. It is their own Spirit.

IF YOU ARE THINKING, 'Well that's a lovely story, but what the hey has it got to do with being an entrepreneur?' A lot actually. Last week I bumped into a prominent businessperson in the city. I had dealings with him many years ago when I marketed some big developments. I happened to ask, 'How is

Ben?' Ben, a friend of his, was one of the smartest, most successful businesspeople I have ever met. A nine-figure powerhouse who owned vast swathes of real estate; he had a big rep. The guy in front of me shocked the hell out of me: 'He's dead broke. He's now in his seventies and he's depressed as hell.'

'What the heck happened?' I asked. He looked at me said one word, 'Ego.' I shook my head waiting for him to elaborate. Finally, in a sad voice he said, 'He thought he could pull off anything. In the end he got into deals that killed him.'

If you think making it is hard, try losing it. And it is way easier to do than you think. An entrepreneur needs confidence, but they also need to listen and realise they are not the master of the universe. I am going to give you a big warning about success and money. It's a 'personality steroid'. Money and success take whatever your personality is and put it on steroids. If you are a generous person, you will probably become more generous. If someone is nasty, then watch out, because the nastiness usually gets bigger when you add money and success. There is nothing wrong with money. Money is inert. By itself it can do no harm. However, if you mix it with a flawed personality, then hey presto! Trouble!

When you are doing really well, everyone wants to bask in your sunshine. I have seen quite a few people believe after years of being on a roll that they are the second coming.

Dangerous ground! Being rich and successful does not make someone superior to people who don't have a bean. Being powerful does not make you 'more' than those who are powerless, because deep, deep down we are all on the same footing. We all have the same power; at our deepest level we are a Spirit—a being.

Here is another truth for you. At the end of your life, you take nothing with you, except the person you have become. All the 'stuff' we accumulate stays here. It is very easy to get obsessed when you are on a roll. Some keep gathering more and more stuff, and that is okay, it really is. It is part of human nature to want more. The danger is when you think that is all there is to life. If we are divorced from who we really are then we look to the outside world to gain happiness. Happiness and contentment come from inside. Yes, the outside trophies and big wins will give us happiness, but it does not last. Some get on the treadmill and keep racing, searching for the next big thing. And that is fine as long as you realize you are already the next big thing.

There is another concept I want to bring up that is the exact opposite of this. It is insidious and has the power to keep you poor and unfulfilled...

The Spiritual Persona That Keeps You Poor

Kevin wafted into one of my seminars wearing flowing clothes and a scarf to match. Approaching one of the other participants, he gazed longingly into their eyes and languidly moved in for the kill. Moving slowly in his deeply 'spiritual' way, he proceeded to give this poor unsuspecting recipient a hug that resembled being wrapped in soggy lettuce. The guy on the other end looked like he would rather be tortured by terrorists and tried to unwrap himself from Kevin the octopus. 'This will be interesting,' I thought. Sure enough, it wasn't long until Kevin piped up with a question about a new business that was struggling. Cutting to the chase, I said, 'Money has always been a problem for you, hasn't it?'

Kevin looked a little startled, but to his credit said that yes that was the case. Then a little defensively he said that money wasn't important to a spiritual person because, after all, everything is an illusion. I smiled. 'Kevin, do you want to have a nice illusion or a horrible one?' He took my half-joke really well, finally admitting that he was miserable and struggling in life.

Now, Kevin is an extreme example, but there are a lot of people who hold deeply spiritual beliefs that keep them poor. Here is a question for you: is being spiritual an experience, or a set of beliefs? Oftentimes with the people who take on some sort of spiritual identity or persona, they may be doing it for reasons they are completely unaware of. It can be a subconscious desire such as, 'I want people to see me as a nice person, a loving person, a kind person and a good person.' In other words, it is a way to get people to like them or be recognized. The problem they often have is they have no 'edge'. None of that ability of the Achiever to confront life full-on, to take on challenges. In fact, a lot of them avoid challenging situations and responsibilities, and it is very hard to become successful if you do that. A lot of them are poor, but secretly so many of them want to be rich.

Being spiritual has nothing to do with an act or a persona. It is going way beyond a persona. Some of the most deeply spiritual people I have met are just ordinary people—yes they are kind and loving but they also do not shy away from life and challenges. And for a lot of them you would never suspect that they were spiritually inclined unless you got to know them well. For them it goes way beyond a set of beliefs and a persona to an actual experience.

What is Real?

Just as we constantly change our clothes, our bodies are also constantly changing. The body you inhabit right now is biologically entirely different to the one you inhabited three years ago. Every cell and molecule is completely different.

It is not only your body that is in a constant state of change. Your thoughts and beliefs are different from those you had when you were a child. At seven, you viewed the world in a different manner than you do now. Have you noticed that what you were so certain of years ago, may now seem absurd? You are probably familiar with the humorous remark: 'When I was 18, I always considered my parents stupid. By the time I reached 28 I was amazed at how much intelligence they had gained in 10 years.'

If our bodies, thoughts, beliefs, opinions and emotions are constantly changing, then we have to ask the question, 'What is real?' Anything that is in a constant state of change cannot be classed as real. From reading about the discoveries made by quantum physicists in the chapter on the Sage, you know just how little is real.

The only thing that is real and unchanging is your essence, your being, your Spirit.

One of the best descriptions comes from Alfred, Lord Tennyson, the one-time Poet Laureate of the United Kingdom. He wrote of his own experience of contacting his Spirit:

"A kind of waking trance have I frequently had from boyhood onwards, when I have been all alone. This has generally come upon me through repeating my own name two or three times to myself silently till all at once, as it were, out of the intensity of consciousness of individuality, the individuality itself seemed to dissolve and fade away into boundless being, and this is not a confused state, but the clearest of the clearest, the surest of the surest, the wisest of the wisest, utterly beyond words, where death was a laughable impossibility, the loss of personality (if so it were), seemingly but the only true life. I am ashamed of my feeble description. Have I not said the state is utterly beyond words?"

What is the point of all this?

Is there a God? What is the ultimate truth? I am not a guru. I have been delving into this area for decades, but I am still a work in progress. All I can say about this is that this section, at the very least, might give you a sense of perspective; it might even give you a sense of wonder and it might even give you the realization that you do not have to get to the top just using your own personal force.

If you are looking for pointers in what to do to deepen this area, I would suggest it does not come from more and more beliefs and fixed constructs. The Bible (Psalms) says, 'Be still and know that I am God.' Big clue there—stillness. Practices that create stillness of the mind.

You can't figure out the Big Questions with your rational mind. The rational mind and science are hailed as the supreme authority. If you go deeply into science you will find strange anomalies that cannot be explained with the rational mind. As I have mentioned before, Einstein said, 'I didn't arrive at my understanding of the fundamental laws of the universe through my rational mind.'

There's a phenomenon called quantum superposition. This principle of quantum physics suggests that particles can exist in separate locations at once. Yes, exactly the same particle can exist in different locations at the same time. Physicists from Stanford have now demonstrated the superposition of a group of atoms at 54 centimeters. Yes, they measure the same particles at 54 centimeters apart—the same particles exist in different locations at the same time. Try fitting that into a rational explanation of the world. The celebrated physicist Richard Feynman said, 'If you think you understand quantum mechanics, then you don't.'

Where am I going with all of this? Individually we are immensely powerful and our ability to succeed using our will is incredible. But anyone who has seen footage of a tornado or a hurricane instantly recognizes there are forces far more powerful than our personal will.

Hey Friend,

That completes our journey for this section. I was going to end the book right here. But for those who want TO BECOME RICH, I have added a whole new section. IT'S A SET OF TOOLS!

If that isn't you—no problem. You can get some great free resources at EpicVideoGift.com

If you want more, turn the page to discover why it is absolutely essential to take the two roads...

So, You Wanna Be Rich?

There Are Only Two Roads to Success...

The way to escape the grind is via two roads—and you need to take both of them. The first road is 'Strategies' and the second road is 'Structure'.

Strategies are the actual techniques you need to use, the specific formulas that you need to make money and become successful. And in this section, we are going to give you a bunch. They are very important, but your structure is even more important.

The easiest way to explain structure is to imagine two goldfish in a pet shop. One day two sisters, Tanya and Rose, walk into the pet shop and they buy a goldfish each. Tanya puts her small goldfish into a tiny little bowl. There is just enough room for a few pebbles and a miniature plant.

Rose, however, has a massive aquarium given to her by her Uncle Phil, who is an expert in raising fish. It covers the entire length of one wall in her room. After a few months Tanya walks into Rose's room and is staggered. The goldfish in the aquarium is huge. Perhaps she's mistaken? She runs into her room and checks. Sure enough her little fish is still the same size as when she bought it. Thinking her little fish is sick, she calls Uncle Phil. 'Tanya,' says Uncle Phil, 'there is nothing wrong with your goldfish. The reason it has stayed small is because it is governed by the size of the bowl. Rose's goldfish is bigger because it had more space to grow because she put it in the aquarium.'

Goldfish grow to a size appropriate to the size of their bowl. If the fishbowl is small, the goldfish will remain small. If we put that same goldfish in a bigger bowl, it would grow.

The fishbowl is the structure, and you and I are much like those goldfish. Each of us has a structure that we live in. It is made up of a myriad of things including our beliefs, emotions, pre-conditioning, mindsets and habits. What we believe is possible in life is very much dependent on the conditioning we received as children and the environment we grew up in. Thankfully, our ideas can be changed in later life by new experiences and access to new information and knowledge, and this allows us to expand that limited goldfish bowl we unconsciously live in.

"We are all living in cages with the door wide open."
—GEORGE LUCAS

Structure is what creates success. Strategies are certainly important, but it's your structure that will determine just how far you will go. Let's get a clearer picture of how our structure works. I want you to try a little experiment with me. Cross your arms across your chest (so each hand is touching the opposite elbow). Which arm is on top—the left or right? Now switch arms so the opposite arm is on top. How does that feel? For the vast majority of people it usually feels uncomfortable. It's because they have developed a habit and that habit has become part of their structure. For example, people who make a six-figure income have a certain structure they inhabit, while seven-figure income earners live in a different structure (same as our goldfish example).

WORD TO THE WISE: Let's say someone wants to be a seven-figure income earner and they currently make $80,000 a year. You can give them a plethora of terrific strategies, but they will find it really difficult to have a quantum leap until they change their structure. They have developed a limited structure that inhibits their success.

Many years ago, I had a young woman in my course called Emily. She stood up and said that she would like to make a lot more than she was currently making.

I asked, 'How much do you currently make?'

Looking rather sheepish, she quietly replied, '$14 an hour.'

Not wanting to embarrass her, I said, 'Hey no problem.' She looked relieved.

'Emily, how much do you think you deserve to make?'

Looking at the ceiling and then at me, she said, 'Well I would like to make a lot more than that.'

I gently said, 'Yes I know you would like to make a lot more, but how much do you think you deserve?'

To her credit she really thought about it, then said, 'The truth is I feel I only deserve $14 an hour.'

Now if you think, 'Hey I'm a high-income earner, that doesn't apply to me,' then think about this: somewhere in her structure was an income ceiling of $14 an hour that limited her ability to move past that point—until she understood it. Prior to that she lived in a 'goldfish bowl' that was small. Her personal level of expansion was small. Here's the question we need to ask: 'Is my income limited to my level of deserving?' Wanting and deserving are two different things.

Powerful Habits, Powerful Thoughts

Your structure is not just about the 'size of the bowl you live in', it's also about the habits you have. Some of those habits, like which arm is crossed across your chest, don't really matter in life. Other habits, such as whether you procrastinate, can have a huge impact on your results!

Habits are just one part of what forms our structure. Our structure is also created by our beliefs. Let's say someone believes that rich people are crooks, or dishonest. What financial condition do you think this person will be in? Logic would say that if someone identifies rich people as dishonest, they won't want to appear dishonest and therefore they are not rich. Because if they were rich, in their own mind, they would be a crook. It is hard to have what you judge! All my research tells me that those people that complain the loudest about money are the ones who have the least, even though they may secretly covet it. These negative beliefs also help create a 'negative' structure.

When we change our beliefs and develop powerful new habits, we dramatically increase our ability to succeed.

I remember one occasion, when I was leading a seminar, I asked the group, 'What's the difference between someone who makes $100 an hour and someone who makes $1,000 an hour?' Quick as a flash, someone yelled out, 'One zero!' The whole room cracked up. Later that night I thought about it and realized that while he was joking, in reality what he was saying was true. It's just a zero. That zero just comes from our structure. If we can learn great strategies and expand our structure to the point that we can use and apply those great strategies, then our lives can change very quickly.

Fly Me to the Moon...

The strategies and structure can be thought of like this: imagine you are an astronaut, and you are strapped into your rocket ship. You can hear the final countdown as your ship prepares to launch for its journey to the moon. You realize the only thing that is going to get you there is this rocket ship. The announcer continues his count, 'eight, seven, six...' You're totally focused on your goal—the moon. A few vague doubts rush through your mind. Will the ship be okay? Do you have the skills to navigate the journey? But you remind yourself that it's too late now as you hear, 'One. Ignition. Blast off.' The rocket moves off the ground, the roar is deafening and the speed begins to build. Soon the ground begins to seem a long way away and as you break through the Earth's gravitational field it dawns on you that there is absolutely no turning back. You are 100% committed to your goal.

All those late nights of study at command central come flooding back to you and all the complex jargon and mathematical equations become clear, boiling down to a few simple home truths. Basically, this rocket ship has two primary sections. The first is the small nose cone where you sit. This is where you punch into the computer the detailed coordinates that will take you to the moon. It is from here that you 'steer' the ship. From here all the 'strategies' that you have learned come into play. However, there is another part of the ship. The rocket ship engine and the fuel tanks are the 'structure'. If you want to pilot your own success rocket ship, then you need cutting-edge strategies combined with an optimum structure.

I think it's only fair at this point to take a closer look at structure in terms of beliefs. What you believe has a very real and tangible effect on what you experience. Your beliefs are developed over time and, for the most part, they will remain subconscious. In other words, unless someone asks you a direct question—like the question I asked Emily about how much money she was worth—you may never actually become aware of what you believe.

As a result of this unconscious element, beliefs and the importance of beliefs have been hijacked by the personal development industry. There are a lot of people who are into the idea that all they've got to do is visualize and they'll be rich. So they sit in a chair for 10 minutes first thing in the morning and last thing at night and think happy thoughts about the money pouring in. They visualize themselves as a rich person and put up countless laminated cards in their shower and on their fridge about being Richie Rich, Rich, Rich. They fill books with goals they want to achieve and the money target they are aiming at, and somehow they think that's all they need to do and everything they dream of will materialize, as if by magic.

While that is useful to some degree, I'm sorry to burst your bubble but if that's all you do, then not much will happen! Your structure goes waaaay beyond visualization and positive thinking. Why is it that someone can be in the same business, doing the same things as the person down the road, and yet be three times more successful? That is our structure—a culmination of our hidden, negative thoughts about money; our core emotions that drive us; the limitations we place on ourselves; the size of the game we are willing to play; and the daily habits we have.

You also need to actually do something. Einstein said, 'Nothing happens until something moves.' You have to move! You have to get out of your chair and make it happen. You have to get creative in your business and stay committed. You have to be determined to persevere no matter what, and you have to be willing to fail, learn and try again. You have to learn to adapt to the signals of success and make shifts in your course so that you arrive at the destination you have been visualizing in the armchair in the morning!

Getting Rich Quick

So many people want to get rich without doing a lot of work. While there are no prizes for getting rich slowly, it is often unrealistic to think it's going to happen overnight. One of the few ways of getting rich instantly is with a balaclava and a sawn-off shotgun—not recommended, unless you like looking through bars for 10-15 years.

Many intrepid seekers of wealth are out there trying to get rich in a nanosecond. They begin to study every single strategy they can on making money in either business or investing, or both, and often not a lot happens. Why? Because they haven't handled something else. Something way more insidious, that is lurking deep within—their structure.

Have you ever heard people talking negatively about money? Have you been part of those conversations? The idea of talking negatively about money is as silly as talking negatively about air. The truth is you need air and, like it or not, you need money. Let's start by looking at the myths and misconceptions that exist about money to help clear them up once and for all. There is another reason this is very important. People that don't have money have lots of these misconceptions locked up in their head, and people that do have money don't. Big clue: do what the people who have money do (AND THINK), and you are more likely to have money!

Myth #1: If you're rich you must have done something dishonest

There are still far too many people who genuinely believe you have to be a ruthless ratbag to succeed in business—that relentless disregard for people in favor of profit is the only way to succeed. If you believe this, even subconsciously, do you think that it might prevent you from becoming rich? I know quite a lot of people who are wealthy and they have entirely different beliefs about money than those that don't have it. As I said, that is a BIG CLUE.

Amongst people who are not rich, there is almost an unspoken understanding that those who are very wealthy must have done something dishonest to achieve such riches. Nudge, nudge, wink, wink: 'Well, yes they're rich, but they have obviously worked over a lot of people to get there. AND they've been lucky.'

Perhaps it's easier that way. It's easier for people to criticize wealth and insinuate that it was attained through dodgy dealings than to face the fact that perhaps someone is wealthy because they don't spend five hours a night on Facebook or watching sitcom re-runs! Maybe, just maybe, that person has money because they had a plan and were determined enough to get off their butt and make it happen!

This myth about the evil of money goes hand-in-hand with the nobility of poverty—apparently the rich are somehow immoral, and the poor are not. The idea that you can be rich and a good person seems totally foreign to some people! But again, I have to question whether that's really what people think or is it just a convenient 'cop-out'. It also makes some people feel better about their situation, if they make the rich wrong.

Whether you were born with money or not makes absolutely no difference to your ability to make it and keep it. There are hundreds of examples of those who were born poor and created amazing lives of contribution and happiness. Money in and of itself is meaningless—it doesn't make people good or make people bad. As I mentioned before, it makes you more of who you are. It is a 'personality steroid'. If you are nasty, or generous, then you are probably going to be more of that. However, by itself, money is inert.

Myth #2: It's immoral to have a lot of money

When people say, 'It's immoral to have a lot of money', what they are saying is, it's okay to have a bit of money, but not a lot. Let me give you a crucial example. If someone were to come along and punch you for no reason, that would be immoral. If they were to shoot you dead, that would also be wrong—but the degree is different and the court would deliver a punishment far more severe than that for being punched. That is how morality works. It is on a sliding scale. Same with stealing. If you steal a magazine from a store, that is immoral. However, if you steal someone's entire life savings, leaving them penniless, it would also be immoral; however, most people would agree it would be a far greater crime. Both actions are wrong, but the degrees of punishment would be different. So based on that, if it is morally okay to have $10, how can it be immoral to have $10 million? If morality works on a sliding scale, then by saying it's immoral to have millions, it should also be immoral to have $10. But that's not true, is it? Why is having a dollar okay and having $10 million not? What makes one acceptable and the other immoral? I don't get that. If that money is made ethically, how can it be immoral? We know it is not immoral to have $10, so why is having millions immoral?

Myth #3: The rich know a secret that we don't

Some people believe the rich know something that the majority do not know. They believe the rich have secret connections and have inside knowledge. They believe the rich know a lot more strategies. Yes, that is true BUT what is way more significant is that they THINK in a completely different manner.

One of my favorite quotes is by the world's first billionaire and philanthropist, Andrew Carnegie, 'I am no longer cursed by the affliction of poverty because I have taken possession of my own mind.' Powerful words! It's our mindset that has an enormous influence. If you think this is my half-baked theory, then consider this: it comes from over a quarter of a century working with tens of thousands of people. Yes, strategies are important, and I teach those, but the really big breakthroughs are nearly always a structure (mindset) breakthrough. One last thing. Andrew Carnegie was the person who inspired Napoleon Hill to write *Think and Grow Rich*. The first word in the title is 'think'.

Myth # 4: You have to be really intelligent to be rich

First of all, being smart at school is no guarantee of becoming rich. Some of the richest people in the world were not much good at school. The kind of smarts you need are the ones they don't teach at school—the smarts that tell you the things that work in the real world and produce real-world results. I have a lot of clients who are not overly educated, and you certainly wouldn't call them brilliant, but they follow the formula I outline, and they have done extremely well. That is what I call smart: doing things that work and not doing what the majority does. Just following the crowd is one way to pretty much guarantee a life of hard work and average results.

Singapore has spent over a billion dollars in researching what the future of jobs will look like. They predict tremendous change and disruption in the labor market, and that so-called soft skills will become preeminent. They believe the old model of getting good grades will be less important, and employers will be looking at skills like the curiosity to seek out new experiences; resilience to bounce back from stress and setbacks; adaptability; and having a very clear insight into your own and others' thoughts, behavior and feelings. If you look at these skills, they are 'structure' skills. And they are not the only skills they list from their research. Empathy, vision, making a contribution, entrepreneurial thinking and pursuing one's convictions will be essential. This is a vastly different model than the old 'get great grades and you will be set for life'.

The Crazy Gorilla Secret to Make Money

An Ig Nobel Prize for Psychology, for achievements that 'make you laugh, then think' went to Daniel Simons of the University of Illinois and Christopher Chabris of Harvard. They asked a group of people to watch a video of a game of basketball. They were asked to count the number of passes that one of the teams made. During the video, a woman in a gorilla suit walked onto the court for a full seven seconds, wandering among the players. At one point the gorilla even turned to the camera and beat her chest! Less than half the viewers saw the gorilla! Why? Because the viewers were so focused on counting the passes that they didn't see anything else, including a gorilla! That is 'Achiever Thinking' and it tends to dominate how a lot of people view the world.

It's the same thing with the rich. They are rich because they focus on money. It's not a happy byproduct of their business; it's the primary target. However, there is something else you need to know. If the only thing you care about is making money, then you won't make much either. I will give you an example. Have you ever tried to buy a used car from a salesperson that only wanted your money? You probably didn't buy the car, did you? You have to make money a target, but you also have to focus on something else as well. We talked a lot about this in the Architect, when I discussed your Success Drivers.

It's the same with anything—you get what you focus on. In a relationship, if you don't spend any time together and don't focus on each other, the relationship will fall apart. It's really not that complicated—if two people don't have fun together, don't communicate or laugh together, then how are they ever going to stay together? And what happens when that focus goes outside the relationship? Affairs happen. It's just because their attention and focus have shifted.

If you don't focus on something, it doesn't happen or it disappears. If you don't focus on your kids then one day they'll be gone and you'll realize you don't know them. If you don't focus on your health, you may pay the price of being ill. If you don't take care of your body and treat it well, it will deteriorate.

It's the same in business! If you focus on adding value then you'll add value, whether it is financially viable or not. If you focus on having the best customer service then you'll keep your customers very happy, even the ones who never pay on time or are more trouble than they are worth. If you focus on money AND genuinely helping people, then you are more likely to make money—as long as you have something commercially realistic. Make it a priority.

I remember Sophia really well. She did amazing work, empowering women. She traveled the world teaching her skills. Her clients raved about her, but Sophia had one very big problem. She was lurching from one client to the next, barely surviving financially. This went on for years. She convinced herself that it was part of the job of helping people, until she met me. Her primary driver was to make a contribution—in fact, this was her only driver! No wonder she was struggling. We talked and finally got down to the nitty-gritty. She did not believe she could make a great living because it would be immoral to charge a decent amount. I asked, if it was immoral to charge a decent amount, then why was she charging any amount at all? (Remember the above conversation about morality working on a sliding scale.) The truth finally dawned, and she saw a different reality to the life she was living. A life where she could actually have a life.

Okay that is the Structure conversation. NOW, let's get into the Strategies of HOW you can make it happen.

Income Strategies

Run the Numbers

If you're going to get practical about money, you've got to have a vehicle that can actually make you money. Let's say I am a barber. I open up in town with a red and white pole and I'm cutting for $20, one person at a time. Even if the store's full all day, that's as good as it gets and I'm working like a dog for not a lot of money!

You've got to understand the vehicle you have to make money and find ways to utilize your advantage to the best of your ability. In the case of the barbershop, you may love being a barber. Using the business model I outlined above, it is unlikely you will make millions and that is okay, as long as you are okay with it. However, if I change the model, then it could be different. Let's say I relaunch myself as an upmarket hairdresser, open a place in a fashionable area, charge a zillion bucks for a haircut and a color and position myself through very clever PR as the hairdressing guru. Then I develop products that are sold online... suddenly it's a whole new ball game. The vehicle has been turned into a Ferrari. And it can get even better. Let's say I build a database of my customers, send them regular newsletters and build rapport. Now I have such great rapport I am able to sell other completely different products to those customers, creating whole new profit centers—and all without doing a lot more work.

One of my clients, a plumber, has such fantastic rapport with his clients that he is now marketing clean-air-purifying systems to them—all done by a simple letter that I helped design for him.

There are two questions you need to ask yourself: Do I have the right business vehicle to make money? Is there anyone else in your line of work that is making the sort of money you want? Because if there is, then it can be done, and the business you're in has the potential to make you serious money too.

On the flip side, there is a word of warning. Often people get excited about the lack of competition in their sector, or they are convinced that there is no one like them in the market and therefore they are onto a winner. Unless you're in some cutting-edge technology company, if someone isn't already doing it there may be a reason for that—and it's not a good reason. If there is no one else offering a $2,500 macramé master class in your area there is probably a very good reason for that too! Ideally, you want to know others are making a real success of doing what you are doing—then all you need to do is do it better! There is an old marketing saying, 'Pioneers get arrows in them.' Of course, there are exceptions to the rule. There are always people who see a gap in the market that no one is on to. You just have to figure out if it's viable.

You've also got to make sure that the vehicle that you choose suits your personality and you're not trying to make your round peg fit in a square hole. I remember a time when I was consulting to a real estate firm. I originally went in to train the staff in sales skills. I was having a conversation one day with the business owner and I asked her why she was doing it. It turned out that she was running her business, her staff and premises, because that was her perception of how business should look. She said to me, 'Well, a proper business has staff and a proper building, that's what a real business looks like!' My response was, 'Who told you that?'

In my mind, a proper business is one that makes a profit— actually makes real money and makes a contribution. And if it can make that money easily, so much the better! We kept talking and the truth was she didn't like working with people and didn't like the responsibility of the staff and the premises. None of the staff were really excited about working there either. On her own, she was a dynamite saleswoman, but she was bogged down by a vehicle that didn't fit her. We got rid of the building and we got rid of the staff, who happily moved on to other things, and now she's really happy and she's making a lot of money. She fell into the trap of trying to fit into the conventional idea of what a 'real' business is. But a business is an entity that makes money. That's it!

The Five Ultimate Ways To Generate Cash

These are the only ways you can make money in a business. Let's talk about how to actually make a business profitable. There are five ways to increase business cash:

1. You cut down on expenses or overheads. Most businesses wait until tough times before they do this. Better to do it when things are going well. If you can eliminate what is unnecessary, then you can maximize profitability.
2. You increase the number of clients. This is definitely an area where the *Nexus Point* is crucial. We discussed this in the Poet. It's the point where you or your marketing meets a client or customer. If you can increase the amount of Nexus Point activities, then you can increase your clients.
3. You increase your transaction price. What I mean by that: say you're a hairdresser and you charge $55 for a haircut, then you raise that to $65. You increase the purchase price; it's the third way of increasing cash in a business.
4. You increase the number of purchases from the customers or clients that you already have. This is the philosophy called maximization. Maximization is all about increasing the number of purchases from the customers or clients that you already have. Say you had a hundred loyal clients who purchase from you twice a year. What would happen to your business if you could sell them something three times a year? That would be like finding an extra 33 new clients! Except new clients have a client procurement cost involved,

which will impact net profit. Selling more often to the clients you already have does not incur those associated costs. If you focused your attention on lifting sales regularity, even slightly, your business could go through the roof.

Don't be fooled by turnover. I hear this all the time: 'Yeah but I have a turnover of X.' What you're primarily interested in is net profit. And a big way of increasing that is making sales with lower expenses—and that means increasing the frequency that your existing customers buy from you. Think of the amount of extra profit you could generate by providing a way that your clients could purchase from you more often. This principle of maximization can be a profit revolution for many businesses.

5. Develop a business that's a saleable asset. You need to know first if you have a business that can be sold. Looking at this, it is clear that not all businesses have the potential to be a saleable business.

Say you are a specialized computer technician. You may be the most advanced computer technician of that type on the planet. But it wouldn't translate into a saleable business. I sometimes call it the Picasso effect. Picasso was very successful at selling his paintings, but he didn't have a saleable business because he was the business. If Picasso left the business, there was no business.

If, on the other hand, you have a business that is not dependent on your expertise or particular skill set, then you may have a saleable asset. But this is something that is best considered

203

early on. If you have already established your business, then you need to turn your focus to creating a saleable entity.

It also means that you will need to focus on systemizing your business and being able to prove that there is a proper business structure in place. A would-be buyer wants assurances that your results are duplicable; otherwise the investment is far too risky. The would-be buyer also wants to know that they can bring in their team and get them up to speed ASAP so that the momentum is not lost in the transition period. Systemized policies and procedures ensure that's possible. Is it possible to set up your business to sell it in the future?

Discover the Secrets of 7 Figure Income Earners.

It's all part of your FREE Bonus video course at **EpicVideoGift.com**

Action Step 1

How can I cut down on expenses? Make a list of all the unnecessary overheads and expenses. Remember—most business owners only do this when things get tight. The best time to do it is *before* things get tight. Trim the fat! (Obviously keep necessary expenses).

Action Step 2

Make a list of how you can increase your clients. Brainstorm this with your associates.

Action Step 3

Is it possible to increase your transaction price on any of your products or services? If so, make a list.

Action Step 4

Is it possible to set up your business to sell it in the future? If so, write down what you need to do to accomplish this.

Action Step 5

Write down how you could maximize your clients. Remember it is easier and less costly to work with your current clients than to go out and get new clients. Burn these three things into your mind: UP SELL, CROSS SELL and REPEAT PURCHASES. Up Selling is getting existing clients to purchase more expensive products/services. Cross Selling is getting them to buy other products/services and Repeat Purchases is about increasing the amount of times they buy their staple product/service. Make a list of how you can do it. Let's explore this more.

Making Money Out of Thin Air

I am going to give you a very specific strategy that some businesspeople have used to win in a big way. To make money without a lot of work or expenses.

One big reason businesses fail is that they refuse to go and get clients. Savvy business owners are often obsessed with getting more clients and that is certainly a great place to begin. However, what if there was another way? Imagine if there was an easier way to increase your business income, without huge debt. And without a ton of work!

I call this 'The Maximization Profit Strategy'.

People often say they want a successful business, but not a lot of them really take the time to think about what that means. If they talk about doubling their business, they often think that means doubling their clients. They think if they double their clients, then they double the amount of money that flows through the door.

Think about the ramifications of doubling your clients—more expenses, often more staff and more admin.

What if there was an easier way?

Let's look at the numbers.

Scenario 1: Doubling Your Clients

Let's say you currently have 200 clients. And those clients buy twice a year at $500 for each transaction (that is $1,000 for each client every year). That makes $200,000 turnover.

If you double your clients that is now 400 clients; let's look at those numbers: 400 clients, $500 transaction price, two purchases a year. That comes to $400,000.

Scenario 2: Maximization Profit Strategy

If we took the original 200 clients and got them to purchase one more additional time, it would look like this: 200 x $500 x 3 times = $300,000

If we added a special offer of a premium-priced product that was $2,500 and 40 of the 200 clients took this up, that would be an additional $100,000.

Add the $300,000 to $100,000 and we have $400,000.

We just doubled our turnover, without adding a single new client! AND if we still decide to double our clients and do the above formula as well, we can see how the numbers dramatically increase.

I am a big believer in working smart—not spending endless hours chained to a desk.

It's all about thinking outside the box!

Getting New Clients

Find Your Avatar

Before you spend one dollar on advertising, you need to find what is called your 'Marketing Avatar'. Let me put it this way. You start dating someone and find out they love gardening and playing video games. You decide to impress them and give them two tickets to a monster truck rally. Bad idea, right?

Obviously, you need to find out what they like and give them exactly that. There is only a tiny fraction of entrepreneurs who actually know what their ideal client wants. If you want to get new clients through any kind of advertising, you need to know exactly what to put in the advertising—to create copy that actually appeals to that ideal client you are looking for.

I usually go into a lot more detail than this, but for the purposes of this book, you need to ask the following questions. This is not something you should rush over. Take your time

207

with it. It is very important. Stand in their shoes and ask these questions in relationship to your business:

1. What do they want?
2. What frustrates your clients the most?
3. What keeps them awake at night?
4. What do they complain about either silently or out loud to their friends or family?

I had one client who owned a plumbing business. He found out that clients wanted above all else a plumber who turned up on time. He offered a guarantee that if his plumbers turned up late, then they would do the job for free. He charged a premium price and pretty soon he was number one in the area.

Remember their problems are your opportunities. Solve their problems!

The Three-Step Strategic Plan

To be successful you need to have a plan or strategy. It doesn't always mean you will rigidly adhere to your strategy. The truth is that as you go along the path you are going to find out that there are twists and turns, and if you spent months developing a very rigid business plan, it's probably going to change within a few weeks of starting your venture. However, to climb the pinnacle of success, you do need to map out a plan. How detailed that is depends on your project.

What I am going to give you is a very powerful but simple formula.

If you have ever played chess, you will know that a poor chess player thinks of their next move. An average chess player thinks one or two moves into the future. An extraordinary chess player thinks way out into the future.

It is exactly the same with people who attain an extraordinary level of success in the world. Successful people think and plan into the future. The easiest way to do that is to use the three-step strategic thinking formula, where you think and act on three different levels.

Step 1. Immediate

Step one is to plan your immediate future. Let's use a very simple example. Imagine you owned a pastry shop. To plan the immediate future you would write a list or create a system where you ordered the flour and the other ingredients to make the pastries. You would organize all the day-to-day details for running the business for that day—you need to have some kind of diary, system or list.

Step 2. Intermediate

Step two is where you plan your intermediate future. These are projects that you want to get online in the next six to 12 months. Going back to our pastry shop—in six months time you might plan to add a catering service to the business or expand the size of the shop. It could also be things like looking at streamlining your systems, getting new leads or contracts.

Step 3. Future

Step three is where you plan your future. This is where you see the eventual outcome of what you started. It is the finished product. For example, you may have started that pastry shop with the sole idea that you wanted to build it up from nothing and then sell it in five years.

If you look at the three-step process, it is very similar to our extraordinary chess player, who thinks of their next move, then the next few moves, and then right out into the future.

So where do you start? THIS IS VITAL: you begin with the final outcome. You begin by looking at the future. To use this formula effectively you work backwards from the future. The first fundamental question you ask yourself is, 'What is it that I ultimately want to create? What would my final outcome look like?'

I find so many people are not working toward a future that involves their own financial freedom. Very few people have an Ultimate Outcome of wanting to get out of the rat race. Most are caught in the grind. They are caught in step one on repeat. It's like being caught in a digital loop—all you ever do is run around putting out fires and getting stuff done—but it is often stuff that will not help you get to step three, your Ultimate Outcome.

NOW here is the BIG thing: if you are clear that your Ultimate Outcome—or what I call step three, the future—is freedom, then you won't make the fatal mistake that most people make.

The fatal mistake that most people make is that most of the tasks in step one, their immediate day-to-day life, are not income-producing tasks. They are not things that create a direct and immediate income stream. Most people are focused on busy-time tasks, NOT income-time tasks. John D. Rockefeller said that most people are too busy to become rich.

I was watching an interview with Sir Peter Ustinov, the actor and filmmaker. He talked about his time in California and the local wait staff's penchant for saying in an insincere voice, 'Have a nice day.' He said with his dry English humor, 'When they say that to me, I just reply, thanks but I've made other plans.' It made me laugh, then think. If all you do is have a nice day in your business, then it is unlikely to lead to step three. You have to have an awesome day. If you win the day, you win the war. It all starts with getting clear on your Ultimate Outcome—then today is about working towards that.

Finding a Mentor Who Can Fast-Track You

Back in the days when I owned my real estate company, I wanted to learn more about the financial world and the investment markets.

At the time, a major investment firm had a hotshot, brilliant, chief analyst. I contacted him, explained who I was, and then offered him a deal that at first startled him before he finally accepted.

Here is what I did. For three weeks I became his personal assistant. I made his coffee, ran errands—you name it, I did it, AND I did it for no money! In return he began explaining everything he knew about the markets. The experience was priceless. I learned more in those three weeks about what REALLY worked than I could have in a year of university. I had a lot of fun and accessed a world that is normally closed to outsiders. I know at the time many people were extremely surprised at what I was doing. To them it was a step backwards from where I was and their reasoning was something like this: 'You are a highly successful businessman. How can you lower yourself to become someone's PA?'

This mentality stops a lot of people from exploring the idea of having a mentor. The ego rears its ugly head and people feel that they won't 'lower' themselves to learn from someone who has a greater skill base than them. This becomes even more pronounced as we get older. As an adult it's assumed or implied that we should know everything and the idea of learning from others seems unappealing.

And yet finding a mentor is one of the fastest ways to turbo-charge your success—in any area of your life. If you want to be financially successful, find someone who has become financially successful in the area you're in and learn from them. If you want to know how to have a long and happy marriage, find a couple who have had a long and happy marriage and ask them how they did it.

Here are some suggestions for finding a great mentor

1. Only choose someone who has been successful in the REAL world. There is an invisible energy that radiates from successful people. Just being around them, you 'get' something. If you went to a world-class sailor, they would be able to transmit the experience, as opposed to those who knew sailing from a book. Be very careful about learning from anyone who hasn't got that. In the end, no intellectual qualification is a substitute for experience. Ideally, they should have both, but real-world results are by far the most

important measure when looking for someone suitable. For example, if you want to be a really lousy golfer, come and learn from me. When it comes to golf, I definitely haven't got it.

2. Find someone who loves to teach and can break it down for you. If you have a mentor that loves the teaching process and loves to tell you how things work, then you will learn so much more than someone you have to drag everything out of. It should be an enjoyable experience for everyone involved, so find someone that really wants to teach.

3. Ask. You would be surprised just how many people would love to help you—if you are willing to ask. If they do say no, keep looking and keep asking until someone says yes. I remember a radical story of someone who wanted to work in a firm under an incredibly successful boss. No matter how hard he tried he could never get an interview with the person he wanted to mentor with. The boss left work one day and walked out into the parking lot to see his car with flat tires. He had steam coming out of his ears until a young man appeared with a pump and explained that it would only take him a few minutes to inflate the tires, and all he had to do was listen to why it would be a great idea to hire him. Figuring that he would never meet someone who was so committed, the boss hired him on the spot. I'm not advocating taking the air out of someone's tires, but you get the point. Think laterally!

Having a coach or mentor is a great way for you to stay accountable to your dreams. Above all, keep learning. Someone once said, 'If you think education is expensive, try ignorance!'

Currently I run a mentoring group. If you are starting out, a lot of the people in my group were once just like you and now quite a few are very successful and supportive of new members. If you are already successful, it's a great place to take your skills to another level. To find out more go to WealthSecretsClub.com

A Personal Note

As I conclude this book, I want to thank you for embarking on this journey with me. I truly hope that within these pages you have found some tools to make your life's journey an extraordinary experience.

I know that the elements have been an invaluable star by which to steer my boat. There always seems to be new lessons for me to learn and I often have to remind myself to stay in balance with all five elements.

Deep down, I am an optimist. I believe there is a vast untapped potential in each one of us. I feel very blessed, because having trained tens of thousands of people on three continents, I have seen some remarkable breakthroughs where people have emerged to a far better and greater life. If they can do it, why not you? I often think of 'the truck test'—if I got hit by a truck tomorrow, I would have no regrets. There are so many people who have regrets for an un-lived life. I think people want to be the heroine or hero of their own story.

Here's to wishing you the life that you really want—where you can be the hero or heroine of your own story.

Your Exclusive Invitation to Join Brendan Nichols' Membership & Coaching Program

Discover Little-Known Strategies That Can Massively Increase your Success

I know how difficult it can be to go out there and be successful on your own.

I have worked with countless people exactly like you who have had a big dream.

I know you can probably do it on your own, however, I also know how much more quickly you can do it with someone who's already been there before you.

- Imagine being part of an exclusive group – at an affordable price! Where you get powerful solutions and your questions answered from my 3 decades of experience.
- A place where you can learn winning strategies to get to the top – faster!
- Get access to my remarkable membership site/app, 100+ video and audio tutorials and how-to manuals, AND... get your questions answered by me. Plus, so much more...

This program has everything you need to be successful!

Discover the specific steps you need to take to create an income explosion... practical, results-driven options. And what action you need to take right now - to get you out of a slump, renew your passion and start rolling toward more wealth and happiness.

Member numbers are strictly limited.

Act now to ensure your place. Go to www.WealthSecretsClub.com